'What's lovely about this ~~book~~... ~~y~~ Clare, but you follow their followers as well, including the story of the Franciscan revival within the Anglican Communion. This is how discipleship works. Those who follow Christ have others follow them. The imprint of their witness is magnified through other lives and inspires us to follow too.'

Stephen Cottrell

'Through simple stories of martyrs and mystics, missionaries and thinkers, writers and others involved in pastoral care and social justice, Sister Helen Julian offers a series of compellingly written and moving biographies. From 13th century Italians to 20th century Congolese, she weaves a rich and diverse tapestry of friars, sisters and Poor Clares, members of religious congregations, housewives and priests – mostly Roman Catholic but also Anglican – saints and 'ordinary' Christians. In providing us with these accounts, Sister Helen invites us to do what Clare advised her own sister, Agnes: "Place your mind before the mirror of eternity! Place your soul in the brilliance of glory! And transform your entire being into the image of the Godhead Itself through contemplation."'

John-Francis Friendship, author and former first order SSF brother

'I really enjoyed this book, which surveys some of the fruits growing on the Franciscan tree through the centuries. It is not a history book, but it is well-researched, and the people chosen for consideration are happily varied. There are some pillars of Franciscan life, beginning with Francis and Clare, as well as Franciscans from almost every period in history. There is a balance of men and women, professed religious and lay people, bishops and doorkeepers, well-known, lesser known and new names, but all are presented in a relaxed style which makes this book easy and pleasant to read. It is an excellent introduction to a wide view of the Franciscan charism and will be ideal for anyone wanting to know about the people inspired by Francis and Clare.'

Frances Teresa OSC, Poor Clare

The Bible Reading Fellowship
15 The Chambers, Vineyard
Abingdon OX14 3FE
brf.org.uk

The Bible Reading Fellowship (BRF) is a Registered Charity (233280)

ISBN 978 0 85746 811 6
First published 2020
10 9 8 7 6 5 4 3 2 1 0
All rights reserved

Acknowledgements
Scripture quotations marked NRSV are taken from The New Revised Standard
Version of the Bible, Anglicised edition, copyright © 1989, 1995 by the Division of
Christian Education of the National Council of the Churches of Christ in the United
States of America. Used by permission. All rights reserved.

Every effort has been made to trace and contact copyright owners for material
used in this resource. We apologise for any inadvertent omissions or errors, and
would ask those concerned to contact us so that full acknowledgement can be
made in the future.

A catalogue record for this book is available from the British Library

Printed and bound by CPI Group (UK) Ltd, Croydon CR0 4YY

FRANCISCAN FOOTPRINTS

FOLLOWING CHRIST IN THE WAYS OF FRANCIS AND CLARE

HELEN JULIAN CSF

CONTENTS

INTRODUCTION

In October 1226, Francis lay dying. He was only in his mid-40s, but worn out by his life of service and penance. Shortly before his death, he looked at the brothers gathered around him. 'I have done what is mine,' he said. 'May Christ teach you what is yours.'[1] It was a characteristically humble farewell from a man who has often been described as 'the little poor one', who called himself a 'lesser brother' and who could never understand why so many people were drawn to follow him.

Clare, the first Franciscan woman, shared this humility and desire to point people away from her and towards Christ. Towards the end of her life, writing to her present sisters and those still to come, she said that they had been called to be like mirrors, in which people could look and see Christ. A mirror doesn't exist to be looked at for itself; its whole purpose is to reflect back accurately what is in front of it.

The legacy of Francis and Clare has left a great gift and a great responsibility for those who believe they are called to follow in their footsteps. The gift is the inspiration of their lives and writings, and the fellowship of their prayers. The responsibility is to discern what is 'ours to do', in our own time and place and circumstances. Between them Francis and Clare set examples of community life, of a deep spiritual life, of care for others in their need and for creation, of pastoral care, of preaching the word and taking it to places where it had not been heard, of simply living in the mundane reality of life and of being willing to lay down their lives even unto death. Their followers throughout the eight centuries since they lived and died in medieval Italy have taken all these examples and lived them out in an astonishing variety of ways.

In this book I want to introduce you to some of these people, in the hope that you too will find your own way to follow Christ in the ways of Francis and Clare. Many of them are officially canonised as saints – they are often the ones who are remembered – but others aren't. I've chosen to share some stories from the sisters and brothers of my own Anglican Franciscan community too, as a way of grounding the inspiration of Francis and Clare in the context I know best and of introducing you to some Franciscans who are not saints (at least not officially). You could think of it as arriving at a party: I'm standing next to you and telling you about the people gathered in the room. Then you can decide who you'd like to get to know better.

I'll begin by introducing Francis and Clare themselves, and then we will go on to various groups of Franciscan followers: the founders of the Franciscan life in the Anglican church; theologians, thinkers and writers; mystics, solitaries and those dedicated to the spiritual life; carers, workers for social justice and peacemakers; martyrs; preachers and missionaries; pastors; and those who simply lived humble lives. Many could of course belong in more than one category – it was with their whole lives that they were following, after all – but grouped together under these broad headings I hope that they can shed light on one another and bring into sharper focus the particular part of the lives of Francis and Clare that inspired them.

As you read, I encourage you also to pray and to ask which is the way in which you are called. An American Franciscan wrote, 'I love reading the lives of the saints, because they show us how many different ways there are to please God.'[2] I hope that by the end of the book you will feel that you have some examples and friends to guide you as you seek to please God, to be a mirror showing Christ to the world and to learn 'what is yours to do'.

1

THE GRACE AND BEAUTY OF DIVINE JOY: THE FIRST FOUNDERS

On a warm summer evening in the Italian town of Assisi, a young man steps out of the crowd and begins to speak. He is dressed in a scruffy grey-brown tunic, held at the waist with a piece of rope, and he is barefoot. Gradually people begin to gather around him, some out of genuine interest, some out of curiosity and some wanting to heckle and mock. Most of them have known him for years; he was born here, the son of a cloth merchant, and had been known for his wild social life with a group of male friends. But now he is preaching about the love of God and penance.

In the crowd is a young woman. She too has heard the stories, though as the daughter of a noble family, living in a grand house on the piazza near the cathedral, their paths have not crossed. But as she listens, something is kindled in her heart, and she knows that she wants to follow in this way.

The young man is Francis, and the young woman Clare, the two founders of the Franciscan way, and this is perhaps how their first encounter played out. How had they reached this point, and what happened next?

Francis was born in 1182, son of Pietro Bernardone, a cloth merchant who was part of the rising urban middle classes. He was baptised John, but soon nicknamed Francesco, 'the little Frenchman', because his father traded mainly with France. He was one of a band of young men in Assisi, popular and generous, dedicated to pleasure. But when he was around 20, war broke out between Assisi and the nearby city of Perugia, and Francis, full of romantic notions about knighthood and chivalry, joined the army of Assisi. Perugia won this battle, and Francis, with many others, was taken prisoner. In his prison cell, he had time to think. Ransomed after a year, it took another year to recover his health, and then he returned to work in his father's business. But he was discontented and once again tried for military glory, this time in Spoleto. While there he had a dream, which led to him returning to Assisi determined to serve God, not human power.

He spent the next year living as a hermit in a cave outside Assisi, praying to both know and accept what God wanted of him. It was the first step in a journey of conversion. The next step, which Francis himself always saw as the real beginning, came with his encounter with a leper. Leprosy was then believed to be highly contagious; lepers were driven out of the towns to live in isolated colonies, and Francis had always been terrified of them. But somehow this time God's grace enabled him not to flee, but to give the leper alms and to embrace him. Perhaps this was God's plan for him. Francis went to live with the lepers for a time, serving their practical needs and sharing the good news with them.

He continued to spend much time in prayer, and one day in 1206 he was praying in the semi-derelict church of San Damiano, just outside Assisi. As he prayed, he seemed to hear the figure on the crucifix over the altar speak to him. 'Francis,' it said, 'go and rebuild my church, which as you see is falling down.' He responded literally and enthusiastically, and began to collect stones to repair the church. When he ran out of money, he took some cloth from his father's shop, sold it and offered the money to the priest at San Damiano to continue the work. The priest prudently refused to accept it, but it was the final straw for Francis' father. He dragged him before the bishop, demanding he return everything he had been given. In a characteristic moment of dramatic symbolism, Francis stripped off his clothes and laid them at the feet of the bishop. 'From now on,' he said, 'I will not call Pietro Bernardone my father, but only God, my Father in heaven.' It was the final and decisive renunciation of his old life.

Francis now took to begging on the streets of Assisi, and when he had rebuilt San Damiano, he moved on to St Mary of the Angels. At Mass there one day, in 1208, he heard the story of Jesus sending out his disciples (Matthew 10:5–10). And, in another moment of conversion, he recognised his own calling too. He began to 'proclaim the good news', and now other men were drawn to join him in his new life of poverty, prayer and preaching. The following year this small band travelled to Rome, where the Pope approved their simple Rule of Life.

Clare was twelve years younger than Francis, the elder of three daughters in the family of Lord Favarone. She was a serious child and from an early age cared for the poor and needy. As she grew older, she refused many offers of marriage. She was 16 when she heard Francis preach, and over the next two years, with just one companion, she met him secretly to talk, and her desire for his way of life grew.

On Palm Sunday 1212 she left her parents' house secretly in the middle of the night and was met by Francis and a few of his brothers. Together they went to St Mary of the Angels, where she exchanged her beautiful dress for a simple habit and laid aside her jewellery. Francis himself cut her hair, and she made a vow of obedience to him. As a woman she could not stay with the brothers, so they took her to a Benedictine house of nuns. Her family were aghast and tried to force her to come home, but when she showed them her shorn hair they accepted that her choice was irrevocable.

Clare's younger sister, Catherine, followed her 16 days later. Francis gave her the name Agnes and took both women to San Damiano, where the first community of Poor Clares began. The life lived there drew other women, as Francis' life drew other men, and the community began to grow. The brothers became the First Order and the sisters the Second Order of this new religious family. Later, Francis would encourage married couples, and those unable to leave family responsibilities, to make a Franciscan commitment where they were, and they became the Third Order (*tertiaries*), often known in those early days as the Brothers and Sisters of Penance.

Neither Francis nor Clare set out to found a community, let alone gain the numbers of brothers and sisters they did. But their passionate desire to follow Christ was deeply attractive. By the time Clare died in 1253, more than 150 communities of women followed her way of life, mainly in Italy, southern France and Spain, but as far east as Prague and as far west as Bruges. Clare could not travel to support these sisters, but we have a few precious letters which she wrote to the founder of the community in Prague, which show great affection and concern for her, as well as wisdom.

Although Francis' life meant he was often on the road, far away from Assisi, while Clare never left San Damiano, they remained close. Francis valued Clare's advice. When he was ill he returned to be cared for by her, and when he died in 1226 his body was taken to San Damiano on its way back to Assisi, so the sisters there could say farewell. Clare lived on for another 27 years, and she was tenacious in preserving and promoting Francis' vision, especially his commitment to poverty.

Poverty can seem a strange thing to value – surely it ought to be combatted? But both Francis and Clare saw chosen poverty as a way of following Jesus Christ, who became poor for our sake (2 Corinthians 8:9). The church was dubious about women's communities in particular not holding possessions and resources, but Clare was determined. In 1215, just three years after the start of her life at San Damiano, she obtained from the Pope the 'privilege of poverty' – the right to live without property or endowments. This was unprecedented, and she had to fight throughout her life to maintain the privilege as the church tried to amend or withdraw it. After the imposition of various unsatisfactory Rules, Clare wrote her own, which contained this crucial commitment, and in August 1253 it was finally approved by the Pope. Two days later, on 11 August, Clare died.

Both communities grew rapidly. By 1217, Francis' followers numbered at least 5,000, who gathered in Assisi for the Chapter of the Mats, so called because they had to sleep outdoors on mats. They were spreading out across Italy, then to other parts of Europe. The first brothers arrived in England in 1224, while Francis was still alive, having walked the whole way. They also went beyond the 'Christian' world. As early as 1212 Francis tried to go to the Muslim world; this journey ended in shipwreck, and on an attempt to reach Morocco a year or two later he became ill in Spain and had to turn back.

But in 1219, during the Fifth Crusade, Francis travelled to Damietta, on the Nile Delta. He set out from the Crusader army to try to reach the Sultan of Egypt, hoping to preach to him and convert him. This was very dangerous; he could easily have been killed. He *was* captured and beaten, but he did reach the Sultan and they seem to have formed a positive relationship. Francis was allowed to preach, but in the end the Sultan could not convert even had he wanted to; politically it was impossible. Francis and his brothers were given safe passage back to the Crusader camp. Perhaps the respect in which they were held is shown in the fact that when the Crusader army was stranded by appalling weather and on the verge of starvation, the Sultan sent food to them. This encounter has become a template among Franciscans for dialogue and relations with other faiths.

A less happy encounter took place the following year when a group of Franciscans travelled to Morocco and were martyred there; their story will be told in chapter 6.

The traditional division between the lives of Francis and his brothers and Clare and her sisters has been seen as that between action and contemplation. Both groups, however, sought to include both dimensions.

Although Clare and her sisters, and the many communities that were inspired by them, were enclosed communities (the only option for women at that time) dedicated to a life of prayer, they were not cut off from those around them. The communities included sisters who were allowed to go out and beg for alms and who would bring back news of the city and requests for prayer. Clare in particular had gifts of healing, and many people came to ask her to pray for them. Their commitment to poverty meant that they had to work hard to sustain their life, growing food to feed themselves, and sewing and weaving items that could be sold for money, which they then gave away to the poor.

More dramatically, when in 1240 the city of Assisi was under siege by a mercenary army, some of the soldiers scaled the monastery wall. Clare reassured her terrified sisters and turned to prayer, praying in front of the sacrament, to which both she and Francis had a great devotion. The army left without doing any harm. Pictures often show Clare holding a monstrance, with the consecrated host (Communion bread) in it, but as monstrances did not come into use until the end of the 13th century, this is artistic licence. The following year the Holy Roman Emperor's troops threatened Assisi and the people called on Clare to help. The sisters fasted and prayed, and that army too left without doing any harm.

Although Francis was often on the move, he was always quick to turn to prayer, and he also spent extended times in solitary retreat. He was even given a mountain, Mount La Verna, by a rich supporter. This was in 1213, and until the end of his life he used it as a place of prayer and retreat. In August 1224 he took a few companions and set out for 40 days of prayer; they stayed at a distance and he settled in a cave. He took a book of the gospels and opened it three times, asking God to use it to show him the way ahead. Each time it opened to the Passion of Christ, and he understood that his way to God was the way of the cross.

On 14 September, the feast day of the Holy Cross, Francis prayed for two graces: that he might feel in his soul and body the pain and grief of the Passion, and that he might feel in his heart the love that compelled Christ to suffer for sinners. Then he continued to contemplate the Passion of Christ, and in his prayer he saw a six-winged seraph (compare Isaiah 6:2) nailed to a cross, and in the seraph he saw Christ looking at him kindly and graciously. He rejoiced that Christ looked at him in this way, but felt sorrow and compassion for Christ's sufferings.

As he sought to understand this perplexing mixture of emotions, something even stranger happened. The marks of the nails and the spear which he'd seen in the seraph began to appear in his own body, wounds in his hands, his feet and his side. They remained until his death two years later and caused him constant pain. Francis tried to keep them hidden and did not want to be glorified because of this gift. These stigmata, as they're called, are hard to understand, and the church often looks upon them with suspicion, as we'll see in later chapters. But for Francis' early biographers they were all about a deep identification with Christ, and the physical suffering was a by-product of this deep love, not something sought for its own sake.

This picture of Francis marked with the wounds of Christ's cross may come as a shock to those familiar only with Francis as the saint of creation. It seems a much darker picture than that of the saint rejoicing in the animals and singing as he made his way through the Italian countryside. But that is also part of his gift to us. Like all of his life, it is rooted in his relationship with God; he loved creation because he loved the creator. And because the creator was Father of all, everything and everybody were brother and sister, members of one family.

This came to its fullest expression in the 'Canticle of the Creatures', which you may know as the hymn 'All creatures of our God and king'. Francis wrote it in an Italian dialect, not the official Latin of the church, and it was written to be sung. Once he had sung love songs to women in the streets of Assisi, but now, near the end of his life, he wrote a love song to God. Surprisingly, it wasn't written as he gloried in the beauties of the Umbrian countryside, but as he lay sick, and in pain from the stigmata and from an eye disease, in a small cell near San Damiano. Because of his eyes, the cell was kept dark all the time, and it was infested with mice.

But in this difficult situation he heard God telling him that in exchange for his troubles he would assuredly receive the treasure of the kingdom. It was in gratitude, therefore, that he wrote the Canticle, praising God for all his gifts in creation. Then he sent out his brothers in small groups; one was to preach, and then all were to sing this new song of praise. In it the moon and water are Sister, the wind and fire are Brother and the earth is Mother. The instruction to 'be praised' resounds throughout the song.

But, as ever, Francis was engaged with the world around him too. Shortly after writing the original Canticle he heard that enmity had broken out between the civil and religious authorities of Assisi, and he wrote two new verses, on pardon and peace, and sent his brothers to sing them to the bishop and the ruler, who were reconciled.

The family relationship of brother and sister also informed the way in which the communities around Francis and Clare organised themselves. Existing religious communities were hierarchical, with the leaders often living separately and more comfortably than their sisters or brothers. But for Francis and Clare leadership was exercised in humility, as a form of service, not as a way of power. Clare, in particular, was radical in her leadership. She only very reluctantly became abbess at all, and she always remained entirely part of her community, sleeping in one corner of the communal dormitory and working with her hands, even when in her later years she was often sick and confined to bed. Her Rule required that important decisions, such as the admission of new members or the incurring of debts, could only be taken with the agreement of all the sisters. At a weekly meeting of all the sisters at San Damiano, the life of the house was discussed and everyone could speak. The abbess and other office holders could be removed from office by the other sisters acting together, and the abbess was to be the servant of her sisters.

Francis' vision of leadership can be seen in the language he used, which we still use in my community. Instead of abbots and priors, there were ministers and guardians, and again they were to be servants of the community. Francis was grateful for God's love and mercy to him, and wanted those in authority to share these same qualities. In his 'Letter to a Minister', he encouraged a minister who was struggling with difficult brothers to love them as they were and to show mercy to them: 'And if he were not looking for mercy, you would ask him if he wants mercy.'[3]

Because Francis' community soon became very large and wide-spread, a different structure was needed from that of Clare's sisters. The brothers could not meet each week; they met once a year initially, and these meetings were huge. As they became more geographically dispersed, it became impossible for all of them to meet at all regularly, and a more representative form of decision-making became necessary.

Humility was to be seen also in how the brothers acted outside their community. In the early days, most worked for others, at least some of the time, and they were to take humble roles, such as labourers or servants, not powerful positions, such as treasurers or managers. They were to be the 'lesser' ones, the *minores*, and in fact the brothers were called the Lesser Brothers, or Friars Minor, the name which Catholic Franciscan brothers still use today.

One of the joys and difficulties of seeking to follow Francis and Clare is that they were often inconsistent – they responded to what was happening in front of them, rather than working out a general principle to follow. It gives their present followers a lot of freedom but also a lot of responsibility.

One example is study. Francis was at times very negative about study, seeing it as against simplicity and poverty. He worried that if books became widespread, it would lead inevitably to hierarchy and even (in a characteristic exaggeration) to one brother sitting on a throne and demanding another brother fetch his book.[4] But when Anthony of Padua (whom we'll look at in chapter 7) joined the friars and they asked him to teach, Francis gave him permission, saying, 'I am pleased that you teach sacred theology to the brothers,'[5] but characteristically added 'providing that... you "do not extinguish the Spirit of prayer and devotion" during study of this kind'.[6]

Clare valued the preaching of the friars to her sisters so much that when the church authorities sought to stop them coming to San Damiano, Clare sent away also the friars who went out to obtain food and other necessities for them. Doing so made it clear that hearing the word of God preached was as necessary as food on the table.

There is so much more which could be told of these two wonderful saints, and I hope that you will seek out more detailed biographies and in particular read what they themselves wrote. For now we move on to look at how this vision, sparked by Francis and Clare, has been lived out by and inspired women and men over the centuries. One much more recent story of that ongoing inspiration is where we're going in the next chapter.

For reflection

- If this is your first encounter with Francis and Clare, what immediately attracts you, puzzles you or even repels you?

- If you already knew something of these saints, have you learnt something new?

- Whichever is the case, spend some time in prayer. Ask as you continue with the book that you may learn 'what is yours to do'.

2

ACCEPTING CHRIST AS THEIR LORD AND MASTER: ANGLICAN FOUNDERS

In September 2011, I had an extraordinary experience. Sitting in the chapel of a Catholic convent in Peekskill, in upstate New York, I listened in disbelief and growing excitement as a centenarian sister spoke of living alongside the founder of my own community.

I had joined the **Community of St Francis** (CSF) 80 years after our foundation in 1905, and Rosina Mary, our founder, had always been a rather shadowy figure. No one still alive had known her in person, and few had even known her second-hand. I knew the basics of her story, and that was all. But how was it that a Catholic sister in the eastern United States had this experience to relate to us? It's a story with many twists and turns, which is not untypical of the founding of many religious communities, including many of the Anglican Franciscan ones. It is very rare for someone to feel the call to start a new community and for the community to come into being quickly and simply. Far more often it's a case of false starts, blind alleys, short-lived experiments and then, perhaps, a community that survives and flourishes – though that isn't guaranteed either.

Rosina Eleanor Rice, founder of the Community of St Francis, was born on 2 March 1863. As a young woman she joined the Society of the Sisters of Bethany, where she made her vows as a lay sister on 17 October 1884. In those days most communities still made a distinction between choir sisters and lay sisters, with the former being the better educated. Rosina was herself well educated, so her membership as a lay sister is puzzling. Perhaps her family could not afford the necessary dowry for a choir sister, or she may have chosen to be a lay sister out of humility.

The Sisters of Bethany lived in Lloyd Square in London, a short distance south-east of King's Cross station. They specialised in retreat work and ran a school for church embroidery. But increasingly they worked in the slums around them, visiting and seeking to relieve those in need. The slums were being cleared and new houses built, and among them was a church, Our Most Holy Redeemer, Clerkenwell, consecrated in 1888. Rosina worshipped and worked there and was much loved and respected by the congregation. Her experience of poverty drew her to the vision of Francis, who was only then being 'rediscovered' by most Anglicans. In 1870, Mrs Oliphant had written an influential biography of the saint, and then in 1893 (with an English translation in 1894) came *Life of St Francis of Assisi* by Paul Sabatier, a Calvinist pastor. Sabatier's book is one of the most widely read books on Francis ever written.

Rosina found support for her own growing sense of being called to a Franciscan community from the curate at Our Most Holy Redeemer, Father John Hawes, who arrived there in 1903. He identified with his parishioners by living on only a partial salary in a run-down attic. Finally, on 21 January 1905, with the permission of the Superior of the Sisters of Bethany, Rosina left Lloyd Square, determined to begin a life of much greater poverty. A few days later she was joined by Sister Hannah, as well as another lay sister and two other women. They were given temporary shelter with a small community of Benedictines in Edmonton. I wonder whether they knew that they were echoing Clare's early days in this.

From there Rosina wrote to the bishop of London, and with his approval the Community of St Francis came into being, by tradition on 25 February 1905, which we still keep as our foundation day. They were invited to Sculcoates, Hull, and rented a house in the dockland area. They took in washing to pay the rent and looked after children whose mothers went out to work. Their life attracted other women to join them, and the community grew.

In 1908 the vicar of St Philip's, Dalston, Father Charles Thorneley, invited them to come to his parish, between Islington and Hackney in north London, and they moved south again. He rented a house for them, writing, in a letter still in CSF's archives: 'It is all in very good repair and only two rooms need much attention. These I have ordered to be stripped, repaired and whitewashed as you requested. For the rest I fear you must accept some "cheerful" wallpapers.' Finances were uncertain; Father Thorneley wrote that he did not yet know whether a grant of £20 he was hoping for would be forthcoming, but 'I still invite you to come. I shall then only have to beg harder. If this movement be the will of God we must not be overanxious for the money. It will be found.'

In 1909 they moved to a larger house in Richmond Road; it had been empty for some years and in such a poor condition that the council had condemned it. This made it cheap enough for them to buy, and they stayed there and in a neighbouring house which they bought later until both were compulsorily purchased in 1962. Their Rule was approved, and the first novices made their vows. They supported themselves by taking in laundry and worked in the parish, especially in caring for the sick and dying. Everything seemed to be going well.

But under the surface Rosina was uneasy. While she was with the Sisters of Bethany, a young American woman, Lurana White, hoping to found a community of her own, had spent some time living with them to be trained in the life. This was in 1897, and Lurana and Rosina had stayed in touch. Lurana returned to America and went on to found, with Father Paul Wattson, a Franciscan community, the Society of the Atonement. Father Paul's dream was of reunion between the Anglican and Roman Catholic churches, and he prayed and preached for this to come about. Out of this desire, he founded the Week of Prayer for Christian Unity, which took place for the first time in January 1908.

There was something of a crisis in the Anglo-Catholic wing of the Anglican church at this time, and it was perhaps especially strong for Franciscans. After all, had Francis not written into his Rule that all his followers must be Catholics? Of course, he wrote at a time before the Anglican church existed, and he was not setting the Catholic and Anglican churches against one another but opposing Catholics to all kinds of 'non-believers' – including heretics and members of other faiths. However, for some Franciscans the tension was too great. On 30 October 1909, the Society of the Atonement, a total of two brothers, five sisters and ten tertiaries, were received into the Roman Catholic church and allowed to remain as a community.

Rosina would of course have heard the news. She waited for another year, but finally, along with five other sisters – most of the community – she sailed for New York. They arrived on 21 November 1910 and went to Graymoor, where the Society of the Atonement was based. They were soon received into the Roman Catholic church and became members of the Society of the Atonement. Rosina Mary took the name of Mary Magdalen.

But Rosina's journey was not yet over. Early the following year she was sent, along with one of the original Atonement sisters, to the Franciscan Missionary Sisters of the Sacred Heart, Peekskill, to gain experience in Catholic novitiate practices. She rapidly felt she had found her true home and entered that community officially on 15 January 1911. She made her life vows there on 25 July 1919, 35 years after her initial vows with the Sisters of Bethany and 14 years after founding the Community of St Francis. She was 56, and this time she really had found her home. She remained at Peekskill until her death in 1946. It was touching to hear that when she celebrated her 25 years in vows there, the sisters kept it as a Golden Jubilee, not a Silver Jubilee, in recognition of her previous years in religious life.

Of the five sisters who came to America with her, one remained with the Society of the Atonement, making her life vows there as Teresa Francis. Three travelled back to England at various times during 1911 and returned to secular life. The fifth, the youngest member of the group, Angela (Alice Witty), was only 20 and was nicknamed 'the cabin boy' by the other sisters. She had wanted to join the group travelling to America, but Rosina felt she was too young to make such a momentous decision. Angela, however, was determined and in fact was baptised into the Catholic church before any of the others – on 3 November 1910, in London. Her family disinherited and disowned her. After that Rosina agreed that she could join the group. When Rosina moved to Peekskill, Angela also moved there and took the name Mary Claudia. She made her life vows on the same day in 1919 as Mary Magdalen.

It was to Peekskill that we had come, as part of a day out from an international meeting of our Franciscan family. We had visited the graves of Mary Magdalen and Mary Claudia and had been warmly welcomed by the sisters. Then we were taken to the chapel, still decorated for the 100th birthday a couple of days before of Sister Frances Marie, and she began to speak. It took us a minute or two to realise that she, as a young sister, had known our founder, and that she was sharing her memories of her with us. Fortunately, someone had the presence of mind to record most of what she said. Apparently Mary Magdalen was a somewhat terrifying person, and the young Frances was scared stiff of her. But once she got to know her, she realised that she was 'wholesome and good'. There is a wonderful picture in our magazine, *franciscan*, of a group of sisters gathered around Frances Marie, beaming like Cheshire cats. In just a few minutes she had brought our founder vividly to life in a way none of us had ever expected to experience.

Meanwhile, back in London, what happened? Only three sisters remained in the community, and only one of them had made vows. This was Helen Elizabeth, who had joined the sisters in Hull in 1907 and made life vows on 6 January 1909. She could easily have given up or perhaps sought another community to join. But she persevered, and although the two novices with her did not stay, other women did come, and the Community of St Francis survived, though it remained small for many years.

This story has been echoed in a smaller and simpler way recently, by the women who have become CSF's presence in South Korea. They too were members of another religious community, but felt called to live a simpler life following the way of Francis. Two stepped out in faith and lived for a number of years in various rented flats, earning their own living and seeking to make the Franciscan life known. It was a life of much insecurity but also joy. Over the years CSF came into a covenant relationship with them, until in 2008 they asked to become full members. The following year they made their life vows. It was the end of a very long journey since they had joined their original community. Since then they have finally been able to build a small house of their own, and another sister has joined them.

The story of CSF has its twists and turns, but it is simplicity itself compared to the men's communities, some of which eventually became the **Society of St Francis** (SSF).

We begin with the Society of the Divine Compassion (SDC), one of five communities that over about 40 years experimented with Franciscan religious life for men, leading eventually to some of them joining together to form the Society of St Francis in 1937. Their histories are often untidy; members overlap or stay only a short time. But between them these groups drew in men who were influential in the Franciscan religious life for a generation or more. Each of their life stories would make a book of their own; I have simply chosen one or two of the most striking characters in each group.

The SDC came into being officially in 1894 when three men, **James Adderley**, **Henry Chappel** and **Henry Ernest Hardy** (**Father Andrew**) made vows, at Plaistow in east London. Adderley stayed only three years, but the other two remained until their deaths. It was not founded specifically as a Franciscan community, but its commitment to the principles of Christian socialism led to a very Franciscan way of life and ministry to the poor around them. Henry Chappel died in 1913, but Father Andrew lived until 1946.

Father Andrew was the first priest to be ordained in a religious habit in the Church of England since the Reformation, and he had an extensive ministry as a preacher and pastor, as well as exercising creative gifts as a poet, playwright and painter. Many people sought him out as a spiritual counsellor, and his books were much loved. He held together a combination of Catholic and Evangelical spiritualities, which has often been seen as characteristic of Francis himself, and in a letter of 1900 he expresses it vividly: 'The very illogical position of holding extreme Catholic views about the sacraments and very broad Evangelical views about the love of God and loving to live the life of a Friar, is the only position in which I have ever found rest.'[7] And much later, almost 40 years after making his vows, he wrote, 'I thank God for every bit of it, the pain as well as the peace, for I know that it has all been God's care for my soul and his patient way of shaping my life.'[8]

SDC may seem to have been a failure – it came to an end in 1952 only six years after Father Andrew's death – but it sowed seeds which came to fruition in a variety of ways. Most notably, its house in Plaistow became a house of SSF and remains so today, still ministering to a poor area of London. Another brother, William Sirr, was given permission to live a more solitary life, and in 1918 moved to Glasshampton, Worcestershire, where he hoped to found an enclosed contemplative community. He died in 1937 with this hope unfulfilled, accepting that he had failed, but saying, 'We must not mind being a failure – our Lord died on the cross a failure.'[9] Ten years later, however, SSF took over the monastery, which remains a house of prayer.

And then there is **Edward Kelly Evans** (**Brother Giles**), who stayed only two years with SDC before embarking in 1913 on a life on the road with wayfarers (his respectful name for tramps). After war service as a stretcher-bearer and then in east Africa, he returned to his former life and in 1921 was offered a base at Flowers Farm in Dorset by the Earl of Sandwich. There he hoped to found a community working to reclaim wayfarers through work on the land, but within a year the community was struggling financially, and Giles was under great stress.

In September 1922 Giles disappeared, and for many years little was known of the rest of his life. However, Petà Dunstan has recently solved the puzzle. It seems that Giles was gay and had been caught in an embrace with a visiting undergraduate. Homosexuality was illegal, and Major Lloyd, a retired army officer living at Flowers Farm with his family, who caught Giles, could have had him arrested. Instead he took him to the railway station and told him to leave and not come back. Until the mid-1930s, Giles was back on the roads, helping out in parishes, having no home of his own. In 1939, aged 60, he is listed as 'incapacitated', and after World War II he lived in a care home in west Sussex, dying there in April 1963, aged 83.[10]

However what Giles had begun did not die with his departure. **Douglas Downes**, who had worked with him on missions to hop pickers in Kent but whose regular job was as a college chaplain at Oxford, was invited to take over as leader of the new community, which became the Brotherhood of St Francis of Assisi (BSFA), though it was almost ten years before the first members made vows. If Giles had not said yes to the invitation to Flowers Farm, Douglas Downes, a key figure in later Franciscan life, would never have gone there; Giles' apparent failure, like William Sirr's, actually bore fruit.

The unique feature of life at Flowers Farm was that the community was composed of both religious brothers and homeless wayfarers; all were called 'Brother'. The diary of the community records that Brother Furse, one of the wayfarers, 'was up before Quarter Sessions charged with stealing gunpowder, fuses and chemicals from the store at the Friary. Brother Douglas gave evidence on his behalf which got him off, and brought him back to the Friary.'[11]

Although BSFA came to an end in 1937 with the union of communities into SSF, its influence was great. Flowers Farm is now called Hilfield Friary and has been central to the life of SSF ever since. For many years it had a ministry to wayfarers, as well as to other guests, and everyone sat together in the refectory to eat. Today it's the home of the Hilfield Community, made up of vowed brothers and others – men, women and children, some staying for six months or a year, others for much longer – who all share in the practical and religious life of the friary.

From Dorset to India. Our next community began as a Christian ashram in 1922. It was led by **Father Jack Winslow**, an English missionary, and was called Christa Seva Sangha. Initially, single men (Jack and five Indians) and married couples lived together as members of the same community. They lived very simply and sought to express Christianity in ways accessible and attractive to Indians. Winslow wrote that the greatest obstacle to missionary work in India was its presentation of 'the water of life in a Western cup'.[12]

Later in the 1920s Winslow visited England and inspired several young men to return to India with him, with others following later. Among them was **Algy Robertson**, an Anglican priest who before ordination had spent three years teaching in Calcutta. He came to India in 1927 determined to transform the Sangha into a Franciscan religious community. The Rule of the community (the Principles) was rewritten shortly after his arrival to reflect a more Franciscan inspiration. These principles were later adapted and adopted by SSF, and then by CSF, and have been hugely influential. In most houses a portion is read every day; they are studied by novices and are deeply embedded in our lives. The chapter headings in this book are all drawn from the Principles.

The Anglican Third Order, founded in the early 1930s, which has its roots in Francis' Brothers and Sisters of Penance, also has its own version of the Principles, adapted to their way of life. And in 1950 the first members of the Community of St Clare, enclosed contemplative sisters, living the life pioneered by Clare, made their vows, and the family was complete.

Algy had never been strong, and life in India took its toll. Early in 1930 his doctor ordered him to return to England, where after convalescing he became vicar of St Ives, near Cambridge. He still saw himself as a member of the ashram, and the vicarage became a community house, to the puzzlement of his parishioners. When in 1934 Jack Winslow also returned to England and the Indian community changed, Algy chose to loosen his own ties to the ashram, and his English group became the Brotherhood of the Love of Christ (BLC).

By this time, conversations had already been taking place between various Franciscan groups, including our final community, the Brotherhood of the Holy Cross (BHC). **George Potter**, its founder, had worked for many years in poor parishes in south London, and the community came into being in the late 1920s as a way of drawing others into this work. It was formally recognised as a community in 1933, by which time its main work was running a hostel for homeless boys.

BHC's house at Peckham was a convenient place for the meetings with BSFA and BLC. In 1934 they agreed a common statement looking forward to uniting, and in 1935 they discussed a common Rule, habit and novitiate. In 1936 Algy moved to Hilfield as Novice Master of the new Society of St Francis, and in October 1937 seven men from the three communities took life vows in the new SSF. BSFA and BLC did indeed unite into one body; Algy resigned as vicar of St Ives, and the two other ordained brothers, Francis and Denis, also became members of SSF, bringing the short life of BLC to an end.

George Potter, however, was more independently minded and totally committed to his work in Peckham. Novices sent to Dorset for part of their training had a tendency to stay there and to change their grey BHC habit for the brown SSF one. In 1941 George Potter stepped back from union and BHC became simply affiliated with SSF. When he died in 1960 the community soon came to an end. Arnold, the last to make life vows and one of those who then transferred to SSF, wrote, 'Father George's personality kept it going. He was an individualist, but a well-loved one. When he died it was only a matter of time for BHC to fold up.'[13]

This is often the risk of a community which has one strong founder with a very particular vision and mission. The transition to the next generation is difficult, and in many cases it does not successfully take place. The strength of SSF lay, paradoxically, in its complex and untidy foundation. Petà Dunstan reflects:

> Most communities had one strong personality who shaped them or a group of founders with a common vision. In contrast, SSF was a community which had evolved, with roots in more than one country, with a host of Religious who could claim to have influenced its development and a 'tradition' full of contradictions: catholic and evangelical; Western and Eastern; traditionally monastic and pioneeringly modern; a priority for the destitute and a priority for mission. This forced SSF to be tolerant of a variety of views and apostolates in its ranks.[14]

* * *

Without then being aware of all this history, I seemed to pick up the need for tolerance of a wide variety of views when I myself joined CSF, which is now also part of SSF. Shortly after making vows, I went to my first General Chapter at Hilfield, a meeting of all brothers and sisters which takes place every five or six years. Four of us were asked to speak at the end. The night before it had rained heavily, and we were washed out of our tents and forced to take refuge on the floors of the guest house. I remember huddling desperately in a corner of the library, short of sleep, and trying to put words into order to say what I wanted to say. And it was about my recognition of our differences and of how we were called upon to listen to one another, to accept one another, to love one another not just in spite of our differences but because of them. The need has become no less as the years have gone on, and can be seen also in the church and the world.

The history of my own founders in CSF and SSF gives me hope that it is possible to bring together disparate groups, to recover from apparent failure, to build something beautiful out of confusion. As Francis and Clare showed, it isn't necessary to have a complete blueprint, just to take the next step.

For reflection

- It seems to be normal for religious communities to have untidy beginnings, with life developing in unexpected ways. How good are you at dealing with this kind of uncertainty? Can you think of a time when just taking the next step, without having everything planned out, turned out to be very productive?

- Most religious communities, Franciscan and otherwise, have not survived. Failure is normal. Reflect on a time when you failed. What did you learn? Can you use this experience to strengthen your faith that God can use apparent failure as a foundation for the future, even though this may not be a future you yourself see?

- Petà Dunstan writes that SSF has 'a "tradition" full of contra-dictions: catholic and evangelical; Western and Eastern; tradi-tionally monastic and pioneeringly modern; a priority for the destitute and a priority for mission.' How happy are you to live with these kinds of contradictions? How might your own church community or tradition be enriched by deliberately including a wider range of spiritualities, ministries, patterns of worship or types of people?

3

THE PURSUIT OF LEARNING AND THE WRITING OF BOOKS: THINKERS AND WRITERS

Francis and Clare were not theologians, and Francis was not always enthusiastic about academic study, but they inspired an important group of theologians and thinkers in the centuries after their deaths. These people (mainly men, as women were excluded from formal theological education) brought particular themes to the fore, and even now it's possible to talk about Franciscan emphases in theology. We'll see that later in the chapter with two present-day Franciscan thinkers and writers.

But first there are two giants – the 13th-century friars Bonaventure and Duns Scotus. My favourite story about Bonaventure tells how, late in his life, he was appointed a cardinal by the Pope. A messenger arrived, bringing with him the sign of that honour, the red cardinal's hat. Bonaventure was doing the washing-up, however, and asked the messenger to hang the hat on a nearby tree until he was finished. I think Francis would have approved.

Bonaventure was born in 1217, when Francis already had 5,000 brothers, in the Italian town of Bagnoregio. He studied in Paris, where he joined the Friars Minor in 1243. In a later letter, he wrote that he was attracted to the Franciscans by their simplicity, which mirrored the life of Jesus and his disciples, and by their learning. From 1248 to 1257 he himself taught in Paris, until he was elected minister general, a role which he held until he was made Cardinal Bishop of Albano in 1273. He died in 1274. As minister general he was commissioned by the brothers to write an official biography of Francis, now known as the Major Legend (legend doesn't imply untruth), and so was steeped in his story. Bonaventure wrote very widely, including biblical commentaries and theological and spiritual works. Of the many themes he covered, I've chosen just two to introduce to you – creation and the human person.

For Bonaventure, creation is best seen as an overflowing of the love and goodness of God. In particular, it shares in the creativity of the Trinity.

> Bonaventure describes creation as sharing in the mystery of the generation of the Word from the Father. It is a limited expression of the infinite and dynamic love between the Father and Son. It emerges out of this relationship and explodes into 'a thousand forms' in the universe.[15]

Despite these 'thousand forms', the universe has order and harmony and hence is beautiful. For Bonaventure this was a sign that creation has meaning and purpose, that it comes from God, reflects God's glory and will in the end return to God. And because it is an overflow of the love of the Trinity, a love expressed in relationship, creation itself is founded in relationship. He expresses in more formal theological terms what Francis expressed in his 'Canticle of the Creatures', in which he addressed the sun as Brother, the moon as Sister and the earth as Mother.

Another consequence of the belief that creation is an overflowing of the love and goodness of God is that the whole created world is theophanic – that is, it reflects the image of God. Bonaventure described how the maker of the world, the holy Trinity, could be discerned at three different levels of expression, with an increasing degree of similarity between the creature and the creator. First came the *trace* or *vestige* – the most distant reflection of God, but found in all creatures, inanimate or animate, from the smallest grain of sand to the furthest star, from the tiniest insect to the largest mammal. Then came the *image*, found only in human beings. Finally came the *likeness* (Genesis 1:26), found in humans who have through grace been conformed to God and hence bear a likeness to God.

This leads to our second theme – that of the human person. We are part of creation, with a particular role and part to play. The world shows forth the glory of God, and human beings are those created with the unique capacity to participate in this glory. God gives us the freedom to choose him and, in that choice, to become like him. Does this seem an unacceptably anthropocentric idea, putting human beings at the top of a ladder created solely to allow them to climb up to their divine creator and making all the rest of creation purely instrumental? It could, but Bonaventure sees the human person at the centre of creation, not the top, with a role not to dominate it but to lead it towards perfection. There is an interdependence here, not a hierarchy.

Ilia Delio, whom we'll meet later, writes:

> The material world is dependent on human beings to attain their destiny in God. We might say that the spiritual destiny of the material world is bound up with the human journey to God. But in return it is the material world that helps human persons find God. In Bonaventure's view, humanity and creation cannot exist apart from each other and attain true relationship with God. Only in mutual relationship is God's love fully expressed.[16]

And Christ, in his incarnation, is the one who perfectly and fully expresses this human response to God as mediator. And we most fully fulfil our destiny as human beings by imitating Christ in his poverty and humility, qualities which Francis and Clare valued highly. This is a good moment to move on to our second theologian, who placed particular emphasis on Jesus Christ in his theology.

Duns Scotus, who as his name suggests was a Scot, was born in the border town of Duns around 1266. He joined the Franciscans as a young man and dedicated his short life (he died in 1308, in his early 40s) to education and scholarship. He taught in Oxford, Paris and Cologne and was very influential in both philosophy and theology. His theology was an inspiration for the 19th-century Jesuit priest and poet Gerard Manley Hopkins. He writes (as does Bonaventure) using the conventions and language of medieval theology, which can make him difficult to comprehend, but there are two key ideas that are worth grappling with, and which still inspire many today to discover Franciscan theology. They are the primacy of Christ and *haecceitas* ('thisness').

In mainstream theology, the fall in the garden of Eden (Genesis 3) brought sin into the world, and as a remedy God sent his Son to be born as one of us, to die on the cross and to be raised, and so to bring about redemption. But for Scotus, as for the broader Franciscan school, the incarnation was far too important to have been simply God's response to something going wrong (original sin). He saw it instead as an overflowing of God's love for his creation – as plan A, not plan B.

The technical name for this idea is 'the primacy of Christ'. Scotus draws on the cosmic hymns in the first chapters of Colossians and Ephesians and the prologue to John's gospel (1:1–18). 'In the beginning was the Word' (v. 1) and this same Word 'became flesh and lived among us' (v. 14). And Jesus, the Word, is also the 'firstborn of all creation; for in him all things in heaven and on earth were created, things visible and invisible... He himself is before all things, and in him all things hold together' (Colossians 1:15–17).

If Christ is the firstborn over all creation, it must be true that all of creation is intended to follow in his steps and be united with him, as he is united with the Father. The incarnation cannot be an afterthought, forced on God by the fall of Adam and Eve. The fall affects the *course* of the incarnation – dealing with sin becomes part of the purpose of Jesus' life on earth – but if Adam and Eve had not fallen, then, according to Scotus, Christ would still have been born, to manifest God's life and love among us and to lead us to a new vision of the whole of creation, one which sees it as the place of God's working. Note how consistent this is with the way Francis and Clare saw creation and saw humanity as part of a family formed and sustained by God's love.

The other key idea of Scotus is 'thisness' – a strange word, but the best translation of the Latin *haecceitas*. He moved beyond the classical thought of the day, in which everything had two components, form and matter. Take a grape as an example: the form is its 'grapeness', and the matter is all that makes it a grape – being sweet and round, having a skin, containing sugars. Scotus took a further step and added a third component – being this particular grape. Now we might find it hard to tell one grape from another and to appreciate the uniqueness of each one, but if we move to something more complex, such as a cat or a dog, we can probably understand this better. And if we then look at ourselves, perhaps we can glimpse the power of this idea. Each of us is unique, chosen to exist in our uniqueness by God and carrying something which is our particular gift, given to no one else.

The ultimate instance of this choosing is the incarnation of Jesus Christ – the Word becomes a particular Jewish carpenter's son, in a particular place and time. And through the gift of this particular life, we are all potentially drawn by God's love to be remodelled into God's image. That was God's original intention, marred by the fall, but now made possible once again through what had always been intended – the coming of Christ as a human being, to show us how we could be.

Neither of these writers is easy to read; they are of their time and use language and concepts that are strange to us. You may feel out of your depth in their ideas. But I encourage you to at least paddle in the shallows of their thoughts; you may be surprised by what you discover.

Franciscan theology as a separate enterprise 'developed in the thirteenth century, culminated in the fourteenth century and dissipated afterwards'.[17] Many ideas which had begun among Franciscans were absorbed into the mainstream, and so it becomes harder to identify specifically Franciscan thinkers.

Franciscans did, however, continue to engage with the thinking of their world. They also had to fight for what they believed and for their chosen way of life, especially when the Reformation brought conflict, dissent and violence to Europe. Our next thinker lived and thought and wrote during these turbulent times.

Caritas Pirckheimer (I confess I was attracted to her originally by her striking name) was born in 1467, the eldest of twelve children of a prominent family in Nuremberg, and baptised Barbara. Her father was in the service of the prince-bishop of Eichstätt, and one of her brothers, Willibald, was a prominent humanist. Humanism at this time was not in conflict with faith, but instead was a movement, centred in Italy, which studied the classical authors of Greece and Rome as a way of producing well-educated citizens able to speak and write with clarity and eloquence. The family valued learning, and Barbara was initially educated at home, receiving a humanist education, which included becoming fluent in Latin. Aged 12 she went to school at the Franciscan monastery of Saint Clara in Nuremberg and entered that community four years later, taking the name of Caritas.

She probably felt very much at home in this monastery, with its large community of about 60 women, all from leading families, and an extensive library and scriptorium. It was a place in which her intellectual gifts could be nurtured and used. By 1500, Caritas was head of the monastery school and also librarian and chronicler. In 1503 she was elected abbess, aged 36.

Her younger brother Willibald went to study in Italy, returning to Nuremberg in 1495. He lent Caritas books and works that he'd translated from Greek into Latin. They obviously found one another intellectually stimulating, and Willibald, who was making a name for himself as a humanist scholar, reported to his friends what Caritas had said in their discussions. This led to some of them corresponding directly with her, and they praised her in their published works. Sadly, few of her letters survive (one which does is to the artist Albrecht Dürer), but the surviving replies suggest she could hold her own in learned discussion, and five of her letters were published in Nuremberg in 1515.

The peaceful and studious life of the convent, however, was under threat. Luther, one of the early reformers, was on the horizon, and as early as 1517 his ideas were being discussed in Nuremberg. Willibald initially admired Luther, and Caritas fell out with him briefly when a letter she had written criticising Luther's views was published in a pamphlet of 1523 without her knowledge. But the following year the council in Nuremberg, influenced by Luther, moved against the two women's communities in the city, and Willibald felt this was going too far and came to his sister's defence.

Luther had himself been a monk and after leaving his community married a former nun, so it was not surprising that he argued against the religious life. He suggested that celibacy was impossible, that women had not joined their convents freely and that they were being prevented from hearing God's word. Caritas, who'd been a chronicler earlier in her community life, started to keep a record of events again from 1524 to early 1526, and then again at the end of 1527. Incorporating letters to and from the city council and her written records of conversations, this record was published in the 1800s as *Denkwordigkeiten* ('Things worthy of being remembered').

A petition sent to the city council in December 1524 reveals Caritas' use of her intellectual gifts to respond to Luther's arguments:

> We can say to your honours in truth that we read and use the Old and New Testament in German and in Latin daily, and that as far as is possible we attempt to understand it correctly... We also know that we should not attribute our own good works to ourselves, but if something good happens through us, it is not our work, but God's...
>
> We also do not despise marriage. For we know that whoever marries does the right thing... In the event that we decide to serve God as virgins, truly no intelligent person can hold that against us.
>
> If, however, someone is not so inclined or does not want to join us, we have nothing against that. We, therefore, do not plan to hold back any sister by force or to keep her from her parents.
>
> We also do not want to condemn anyone, but let every man judge himself; everyone will be judged when we all come before God's judgement. But just as we do not want to force anyone, we also do not want to be forced, but instead we want to be free in spirit, not body.[18]

The council were not moved by these arguments and in March 1525 announced the conversion of the whole city to Lutheranism. They refused to allow Catholic priests to serve the women's communities, and the loss of the sacraments must have been a serious deprivation. The following week, Lutheran preachers were assigned to the nuns, and later Caritas records (with what I can't help but feel is a sigh), 'We have now heard 111 of these sermons.'

In June 1525 the city authorities made five demands: that Caritas should release her sisters from their vows (which of course she had no power to do); that all were free to leave, and that parents could insist their daughters left; that they dressed in secular clothes not habits; that the grilles be removed and ordinary windows put in, so that anyone could speak to a sister alone; and that they should make an inventory of all they owned and give it to the council. A week later, the families of three sisters, aged 20, 21 and 23, insisted they returned home. Caritas wrote a moving account:

> With many tears we removed their veils and girdles and put shirts and worldly girdles and headwear on them... The children embraced me, wept loudly and begged that I not let them go. But unfortunately I could not help them. I withdrew with the other sisters and left the poor children alone in the chapel.[19]

When their mothers arrived, they promised them good things and then threatened them, but the women would not leave of their own accord. Finally, they were pushed or carried outside and put into coaches, still crying out that they were suffering abuse and injustice, but the city police were present and no one came to their aid.

This violence seems to have sobered everyone, and for a while the council acted more moderately. Caritas even had a meeting with Philipp Melanchthon, a leading reformer, and they agreed on most matters, except on the value of vows. Her ability to hold her own in such a debate is striking. Yet the council continued seeking to close the community down, and in 1527 the sisters received a huge backdated tax bill, forcing them to plead for extra time in order to sell some of their possessions to raise the money.

Caritas died in 1532, aged 65. The eventual decision of the council of Nuremberg was that the sisters of Saint Clara's were allowed to remain until their deaths but no new novices were to join, which led inevitably to the end. By 1591 the monastery church had become a (Protestant) parish church, and the cloister was the city's pawn house.

Anglican Franciscans have not on the whole been counted among the theologians, but one exception is the 20th-century New Testament scholar **Barnabas Lindars**. Barnabas spent many years teaching biblical theology in Cambridge, as well as ministering at St Bene't's church, which the Cambridge brothers ran. For the last twelve years of his academic life, from 1978 to 1990, he was a professor at Manchester University, living away from a friary but always very much part of the life of the community. When he retired, he moved to Hilfield Friary, continuing to work on a major commentary on the book of Judges alongside playing a full part in the life of the house. He died in 1991, and the manner of his death reminds me of the story of Bonaventure and the cardinal's hat. Barnabas had gone to visit a resident of the friary in a nursing home, and to save someone the trouble of coming to collect him had said he would walk the four miles home. When he didn't arrive, the brothers went out to search for him and found that he had died on the way back.

Our Principles speak of those who 'give themselves to the pursuit of learning and the writing of books', and Barnabas was one of a small number who followed that path.

Franciscan theology became absorbed in the mainstream for a number of centuries, but recently it has begun to re-emerge. Some of its themes, such as the valuing of creation, are particularly relevant to today's concerns, and its 'alternative orthodoxy' in such areas as the incarnation is attractive to those who struggle with some parts of mainstream theology.

The final two people I want to introduce you to are Ilia Delio and Richard Rohr, present-day Franciscans who seek to make Franciscan thinking available and accessible to a wider audience. Both are Americans and Catholics, but their teaching is attractive throughout the world and across many churches. Delio is the more academic of the two, while Rohr's books appeal to a more popular audience, but both are passionate about making the riches of the Franciscan tradition available to today's world.

Ilia Delio, baptised Denise, was born in 1955 in New Jersey and followed a scientific path, through degrees in biology and a doctorate in pharmacology. She was about to start a postdoctoral fellowship at a prestigious university when she read Thomas Merton's *The Seven Storey Mountain*,[20] and his story rekindled her own desire for the contemplative religious life. In 1984 she joined the Carmelites, an enclosed contemplative order, and took the name Ilia, the Greek feminine translation of Elijah. She made vows there, but after four years she began to have doubts about her choice and asked to experience another community. This time it was a Franciscan community, the Franciscan Servants of the Holy Child Jesus, and she chose to start all over again with them.

Her new community sent her to study theology in New York. She discovered Bonaventure and wrote her doctoral dissertation on him. She also encountered the work of the Jesuit theologian Pierre Teilhard de Chardin, a mystic and scientist. He developed the idea of evolutionary Christianity, by which he meant that the whole of creation was progressing towards fulfilment in Christ. Combining theology with her earlier scientific vocation has shaped Delio's life ever since.

After so many centuries when women could not access high-level theological education, Delio has spent most of her life in the academic world, teaching church history, spirituality and Franciscan studies, as well as writing numerous books and speaking extensively. Since 2005 she has belonged to a new Franciscan community, the Franciscans of Washington DC, who are trying to find new ways of living the vowed Franciscan life in the 21st century.

Delio has continued to study Bonaventure and to draw on his insights, with a determination to make them relevant to today's world. In the introduction to her book *The Humility of God*, she writes:

> Bonaventure's Christ-centered mysticism is relevant to the search for God today in a fast-paced, scientific world that, in many ways, views God as an unnecessary hypothesis. Every theology is a lens of interpretation, a way to view the

deep connections between God and creation with Christ as center. Because his synthesis is 'Christ-centered' it impels us to recognize the significance of the humanity of Christ for understanding the God-world relationship.[21]

Richard Rohr was born in 1943 in Kansas, to a family of German origin, and joined the Franciscan friars in 1961. In 1970 he was ordained a priest and also completed his master's degree in theology. The timing was significant, as many of his teachers were formed by the Second Vatican Council in the mid-1960s, which opened up Catholic teaching and practice to new ideas. Although later developments have sometimes seemed to reverse this process, Rohr remains committed to it. In a reflection written for his 75th birthday, in March 2018, he says:

> We were not so much taught theological conclusions as the process of getting there. I received a full history of the development of Christian ideas more than Catholic apologetics. Little did I imagine how this would affect my entire life and my own approach to theology. The inspired documents of Vatican II put the Gospel back at the center of our lives, just as St Francis tried to do. This made spirituality so much more alive and real than the narrow churchiness I grew up with.[22]

Rohr often describes his position as 'on the edge of the inside' – remaining a member of the church while able to explore outside it and connect with those there. As Delio connects theology with science, Rohr connects spirituality and social justice. Shortly after his ordination, he founded the New Jerusalem Community, an intentional community of lay people in Cincinnati, including families. Then, in 1986, he founded the Center for Action and Contemplation (CAC) in New Mexico, where he continues to live and work. This combination of action and contemplation is very Franciscan – Francis' life was shaped by periods of withdrawal for prayer, followed by intense periods of action, including preaching and service to others. CAC seeks to bring together these two dimensions to enrich and support each other. The breadth of Rohr's vision and his willingness to engage with and draw from non-Christian thought have brought him criticism. But there are also many who find in his acknowledgement of their real and pressing questions inspiration to carry on as members of their church. He has written many books and has an extensive teaching ministry. Some books are specifically Franciscan, some are less obviously so, but all are informed by his Franciscan formation and commitment.

In a review of one of Rohr's more Franciscan books, *Eager to Love: The alternative way of Francis of Assisi*, Dana Greene sums up the message of Francis in words which could also apply to Richard Rohr.

> The message of Francis, the saint, offers an alternative way of life, one anchored in a sacramental understanding of the world, an appreciation of contemplation as a different way of knowing, a wisdom that is nondualistic, and a pedagogy that teaches through living and being rather than through creedal affirmation.[23]

Richard Rohr, in his accessibility, is a good person with whom to end this chapter, and his focus on contemplation leads us naturally to our next group of Franciscans, those who prayed and focused on the spiritual life.

For reflection

- Caritas Pirckheimer in her day and Richard Rohr and Ilia Delio in ours all engage with the thought of their time, seeking to integrate it with their life of faith. To what extent do you do this for yourself? Are there areas of thought that you see as totally incompatible with faith, and others that are valuable and life-giving? Can you extend the boundaries of your willingness to engage? Perhaps you might commit yourself to reading one book which expands your horizons in this area.

- Caritas called her chronicle 'Things worthy of being remembered'. What would you put in a chronicle of your own life or the life of your church or community? You may choose to make this a project for your next retreat or something your church could take on together as a way of recording its story.

- Do you naturally use your powers of thought in your spiritual life, finding theology a spur to prayer and worship? Or does it turn you off and make you feel more distant from God? If the latter, how might you gently move to make fuller use of this God-given faculty? You may be helped by studying with others or by working with someone who can guide your reading and reflect with you on what you learn.

- Bonaventure saw creation as reflecting the image of God. Is there a part of creation in which you can readily see or feel God's presence? For many people this is the mountains or the sea. In a time of prayer, try to extend this sense to other parts of creation, less dramatic but no less created and loved by God. If you can, sit outside, gazing on a flower or tree. If you can't do that, find a picture and use it as a focus. Continue to return to this exercise as often as you like, experimenting with different parts of creation, even those you don't like, such as spiders or wasps.

4

THE SOUL'S ASCENT TO GOD: MYSTICS AND SPIRITUAL WRITERS

While women were often tangential to the theological enterprise, as discussed in the previous chapter, in the area of prayer, mysticism and the intense spiritual life they take centre stage. Ilia Delio sees them as the heirs of the Franciscan theological tradition, which was absorbed into the mainstream and lost some of its particularity. She writes:

> It did survive 'underground' in the voices and intense spiritual lives of Franciscan women. Mystics such as Clare of Assisi, Angela of Foligno, and Veronica Giuliani faithfully carried on an authentic Franciscan tradition of theology rooted in the good. By this I mean that their reflection of God as love led to the transformation of their lives and the world around them.[24]

Margaret Carney suggests that the influence may have worked both ways: what male theologians wrote became incarnate in 'the mystical experience or charitable endeavours' of Franciscan women, but she also asks 'whether the primary influence was the female voice calling the male counterpart to an awareness that enhanced his ministry of preaching and his personal experience of prayer?'[25]

We start with **Angela of Foligno**, a woman who was described as a teacher of theologians because of her advice and guidance to many, both men and women, religious and lay. What she said and wrote came out of her own deep experiences, which were recorded by her cousin, Arnaldo, a Franciscan friar. At this time, reading and writing were distinct skills, and many who could read could not also write.

Angela was born in Foligno around 1248, to a well-to-do family. Foligno is not far from Assisi, and it had a church run by Franciscans. Until her late 30s, Angela was only conventionally religious. She was married young, had several sons and cared for her ageing mother. Something (we don't know what) set her on the path to conversion, beginning with a sense of her own sinfulness. She later recorded the entire story in a set of clear stages in the *Memorial*, though it's likely that these stages were a literary device rather than exactly how the four-year process of her conversion played out.

To begin with she still had her family. But in a plague in 1288, her husband, sons and mother all died. Shockingly Angela had already prayed to be free from all attachments, even those to her family and relatives, and she saw these deaths as a fulfilment of her prayer, freeing her to give herself entirely to Christ. Later she did admit to feeling great pain at these deaths, but this episode is an uncomfortable reminder of the way in which some are called to renounce even family ties. Francis, after all, renounced his father, and Clare fled her family home to follow him. Angela was walking in their footsteps. Around 1291 she joined the Brothers and Sisters of Penance, and Arnaldo came to live at Foligno and work with her to record her mystical experiences. He also helped her to reflect on her experiences and so to grow in self-knowledge.

But her life was not entirely given to prayer. She also ministered to the poor and the sick, especially at a local hospital. When she could not supply their needs herself, she would go out to beg. Other women and men gathered around her, seeking her spiritual guidance, and those further away wrote to her. Because she had experienced love and family life and difficulties and bereavement, she was able to empathise with and advise a wide range of people.

A group of lay women began to live together with her in an informal religious community without taking vows and helped in her service to those in need.

For Angela the Passion of Christ was central, and she spent a lot of time gazing on the crucifix and agonising over her sins, which had led Christ there. As with much medieval spirituality, this can be hard for us to read; it seems overly emotional, leading to excessive penance and self-hatred. Certainly this was part of Angela's experience, but she also experienced great joy through this prayer:

> Once I was at Vespers and was gazing at the cross. And while I was thus gazing at the cross with the eyes of my body, suddenly my soul was set ablaze with love; and every member of my body felt it with the greatest joy. I saw and felt that Christ was within me, embracing my soul with the very arm with which he was crucified.[26]

Even more poignantly, one Holy Week she was meditating on the death of Christ and seeking to empty herself of everything which might distract her. Then, she records:

> Suddenly, while I was engrossed in this effort and desire, a divine word sounded in my soul: 'My love for you has not been a hoax.' These words struck me a mortal blow… Seeing in him all the deeds of true love, I understood the perfect truth of what he had said, that his love for me had not been a hoax, but that he had loved me with a most perfect and visceral love.[27]

Angela also showed theological insight in her reflection on her words. In one of her *laude* (we'll see more of these when we meet Jacopone da Todi), she wrote:

> *I praise you God my beloved;*
> *I have made your cross my bed.*
> *For a pillow or cushion,*

I have found poverty,
and for other parts of the bed,
suffering and contempt to rest on.[28]

When she was asked to explain this metaphor of the bed, she said, 'This bed is my bed to rest on because on it Christ was born, lived and died. Even before man sinned, God the Father loved this bed and its company (poverty, suffering and contempt) so much that he granted it to his Son.'[29]

Recall Duns Scotus and his theology of the primacy of Christ, and see how Angela is already moving towards that theological development. She was not simply a great mystic, but also a deep thinker.

Despite the agonies of her meditation on the Passion of Christ, she also received great consolation. Once at the Eucharist, she heard Mary telling her that in being there she was receiving the blessing of Jesus. And then Mary added her own blessing, telling Angela: 'Work with all your might at loving, for you are much loved, and you are called upon to attain something infinite.'[30]

In her life and in her books, Angela of Foligno did achieve something infinite: the record of a second-generation Franciscan inspired by Francis to a life of prayer, penitence, poverty and service, and sharing also in his joy.

Jacopone da Todi is another second-generation Franciscan, and, even more than Angela of Foligno, he experienced life's ups and downs. A brief summary describes him as 'poet, notary, widower, penitent, friar and political prisoner'.[31] Born Jacopo dei Benedetti in the 1230s, not long after the death of Francis and while Clare was still alive, he came from a financially struggling aristocratic family. He studied at the University of Bologna and followed his father in becoming a notary, a profession that combined elements of law and accountancy. He married Vanna di Bernardino, whose aunt was a member of the community at San Damiano. Jacopo's reputation was mixed – he was successful, but he was also extravagant and indifferent to faith, and he valued wealth and influence over a good name.

In 1268, only a year after his marriage, tragedy struck. While he and his wife attended a public tournament, part of the grandstand collapsed and Vanna was killed. When Jacopo rushed to her side, he discovered that she had been wearing a hair shirt under her glamorous clothes and realised that she had been performing penance for his sake.

Shocked to the core and grieving deeply, Jacopo dramatically changed his life. He abandoned his career, gave away all his possessions and became a wandering penitent. His behaviour was extreme, and this is when he became known as Jacopone – Crazy Jim – a name he embraced. For example, he crawled around the public square of Todi on all fours, wearing a saddle and bridle, and came to a wedding at his brother's house tarred and feathered. It's hard to tell how much of his behaviour was genuine madness caused by grief and how much was designed, like some of the acts of the Old Testament prophets, to make a dramatic point. Another recorded act seems more like the latter – when one of his fellow citizens asked Jacopone to carry home a pair of capons, he took them instead to the man's family tomb, saying this was his true home.

After about ten years of this life, Jacopone asked to join the Franciscan friars. Knowing his reputation, they were dubious about accepting him, but when Jacopone wrote a beautiful poem about the vanities of the world, they were convinced. In humility he chose to live as a lay brother, not as a priest.

It is his poems that are Jacopone's lasting legacy. Known as *laude* or 'lauds', they are devotional poems, expressing his passionate love of God. Jacopone stood in a rich tradition in writing them, as they stemmed from Italian lay religious movements from the late eleventh century. These people, caught up in revival, wanted songs in their own language that expressed their own relationship with God. They were not satisfied with the Latin music and words of the official liturgy of the church. Francis' 'Canticle of the Creatures', written in early Italian, is an example of this kind of music, which was often sung at Franciscan public gatherings.

A total of 93 of Jacopone's lauds survive. Some were undoubtedly written to be sung publicly, but others are more personal. None are dated, and it is not possible to attach them to events of Jacopone's life, but they do give evidence of his passionate and forthright character. Common themes include 'the ecstatic love of God manifest in his self-emptying into human flesh, the madness of God-in-Christ suffering on the cross for ungrateful humanity, the annihilating effect of divine love in the soul who does respond to it'.[32] One of them begins:

> *I know well, O highest wisdom,*
> *that if I am mad, it is your doing –*
> *this dates from the day I surrendered myself to Love,*
> *laid aside my old self and put on you*
> *and was drawn – I know not how – to new life.*[33]

His new life was not, however, free from the difficulties that had marked his earlier life. This was a time of conflict in the church, which affected also the Franciscan friars, who were divided into two groups. Jacopone took the side of the Spirituals, who sought to return to the simplicity and austerity of the life of the early brothers. They were given permission to do so, by living separately, in 1294 by Pope Celestine V, but he died before the necessary steps were taken to bring about the separation. His successor, Boniface VIII, was not willing to support the move, and in 1297 Jacopone was one of those who signed the Longhezza Manifesto, which challenged whether the Pope had been validly elected. Not surprisingly, the Pope did not take this well. The conflict became political as well as religious and ended in the siege of Palestrina and a papal victory. In 1298 Jacopone was imprisoned in the fortress above the town and excommunicated. He continued to write poems, some of which are very touching; others, however, are vitriolic in their condemnation of his opponents – his fiery character remained 'unconverted'.

Jacopone was finally freed in 1303, when Boniface died. His health badly affected by his imprisonment, Jacopone spent the remaining three years of his life living quietly, ending up with a small group of friars living alongside the Poor Clare monastery of Collazzone. He died there in 1306, late on Christmas Eve, while the Midnight Mass was being celebrated.

Jacopone's life may seem far from ours, from a very different church and with an extreme character and experiences few of us could (or would wish to) emulate. But his passionate embrace of God in the face of grief and loss and his commitment to his vision of the Franciscan life through all the troubles it brought him are examples of total self-giving. David Bryant writes:

> Our love of God is often passing, lacking fire and resolution; Jacopone reveals something different that is dynamic and exhilarating, riding roughshod over life's troubles. It is unquenchable... Jacopone describes it with elation: 'Amiable, delectable love, love inconceivable and beyond conception! Love, divine fire, playful, laughing love, never stinting, giving lavishly.'[34]

Camilla Battista da Varano's life began inauspiciously. Born in 1458, she was the child of Cesare da Varano, Duke of Camerino in Italy, and his mistress. Fortunately, the Duke did not abandon his illegitimate daughter, but raised her at his court and ensured she had a good education. He hoped she would make a politically advantageous marriage, but she struggled with a sense of vocation to become a Poor Clare. In 1481 she joined their community in Urbino; three years later, her father, now reconciled to her plans, brought her back to Camerino to found a new Poor Clare monastery there. Two written works, *The Spiritual Life* and *The Mental Sufferings of Jesus*, give us glimpses of her intense spiritual life, centred around following Christ, poor and crucified. It could be strongly affective; she longed to 'leave the prison of the body to be with Christ'.[35] While praying one day, in great sorrow, 'it seemed to me that the blessed Christ was showing me great compassion, and with his arm was hugging my soul to his most holy breast, saying repeatedly, "Don't cry so much." And with his other hand he dried the tears of my soul.'[36]

Her own life brought suffering. In 1502 papal forces captured Camerino and executed her father and brothers, and she fled to another monastery until she felt it was safe to return. She helped to found several other Poor Clare monasteries and died of plague in 1524.

If Camilla Battista's spirituality seems somewhat alien to us, **Veronica Giuliani**'s will probably seem even more so. Another Poor Clare, born in 1660, she was called Ursula but was given the name Veronica when she joined her community aged 17 in Citta di Castello in Umbria (Francis' home region). She lived there until her death in 1727. She served as novice mistress and then as abbess, with common sense and great determination. She had water piped inside the monastery and enlarged her sisters' rooms. She kept a diary, in 44 volumes, and wrote letters, poems and autobiographical reports, from which we learn about her great devotion to Christ crucified. In her 30s this devotion took physical form in her body, as it had done in Francis himself. First the marks of the crown of thorns appeared on her forehead, and then three years later the five wounds of crucifixion on her body.

The church was suspicious of these manifestations. The bishop removed her from the life of her community and had her constantly watched, but he concluded that these were genuine spiritual gifts and allowed her to return to her monastery. Her community name 'Veronica' means 'true image', and her devotion had led her to become a 'true image' of Christ crucified.

Veronica's spirituality was very much of her day, and some of her accounts are genuinely disturbing. She fasted on bread and water for three years, after spending some time trying to get permission for this penance. During that time, she was forced to try to eat normally but was constantly sick, and it's hard not to think that she had some sort of eating disorder. She wrote vividly of assaults by demons, and at one time wrote several prayers in her own blood, from a wound close to her heart. It is easy to come up with psychological explanations for her behaviour, but we are all children of our age, and perhaps our own spiritual practices will not all stand the test of time either. Veronica didn't always understand herself, writing of 'crazy things that love made me do'.

Although she spent her entire adult life within an enclosed monastery, Veronica had a great missionary impulse, expressed in the only way possible for a woman of her time – in prayer. She dreamt of converting the whole world and wrote that she used to say:

> Get up all you creatures, come with me to Jesus. There is no end to the blessings he brings. If you want treasures, Jesus is the true treasure, without measure. If you want riches, Jesus is true wealth. If you long for tastes and pleasures, Jesus is the height of savour and contentment. In a word, if you long for every good, stay close to Jesus, because he is everything.[37]

Almost three centuries after her death, Veronica's missionary impulse was fulfilled in an unexpected way. A religious brother from Lebanon, Brother Emmanuel, discovered her writings in 1994, while he was living at a monastery in Syria, and developed a great devotion to her. In 2016, on 9 July, the first church outside Italy dedicated to Veronica Giuliani was consecrated in Qsaibe, Lebanon, 30 minutes east of Beirut. Next to the church is the house of a new religious order, founded in 2015.

Another saint who came under suspicion by the church was **Joseph of Cupertino**. He seems a very unlikely candidate for sainthood; born to poor but devout parents, he tended to 'space out' of conversations and seemed to be in a trance, which didn't help him in his desire to join the Franciscan friars. Eventually, however, he was accepted and even managed to be ordained as a priest, despite being a terrible student. The story is told that the earlier candidates had so impressed the bishop that when Joseph came before him, he asked him only a few simple questions.

Joseph's trances continued as a friar, and when he was 27, he levitated for the first time. Far from seeing this as a sign of God's special favour, his superiors moved him from place to place to avoid the crowds who flocked to see 'the flying friar'. At least 70 levitations are recorded, and witnesses to them ranged from the faithful and his brother friars to scientists and a pope, Urban VIII. He was suspected of being a fraud and a witch and was investigated by the Inquisition, who exonerated him.

What made him a saint, however, are not these extraordinary acts but the humility, obedience and patience with which he bore all the difficulties of his life, as well as his dedication to prayer. Perhaps inspired by his levitations, he wrote that we must soar in spirit, to glorify God Most High by our holy deeds. Joseph of Cupertino is a reminder that true wisdom comes from God and can seem to be foolishness. As the apostle Paul wrote, 'For God's foolishness is wiser than human wisdom, and God's weakness is stronger than human strength' (1 Corinthians 1:25).

Joseph died in 1663 and was declared a saint a century later. He is popular as the patron saint of students who are struggling, especially with exams, and also more recently as the patron of airline travellers, though I'm uncertain whether someone who could fly without need of an aeroplane is quite the right person for this role!

Inevitably most saints of earlier centuries are European, but now we move to Africa, to meet a young woman from the Congo. **Claire of the Eucharist** was born in 1960 and lived only until 1984, when she died of cancer. But her story is a powerful one, of God's grace and of a life turned around.

Born Muambule Tchipanga in Kabinda, she was the oldest child of a large family and her father's favourite. Her father had been a Catholic, but because he wanted to marry more than one wife and have many children, he had founded his own church. In the end he had four wives and 20 children. His daughter was very strong-willed, and her father's preference for her over his other children did her no favours; she was proud and determined to have what she wanted. This made her unpopular with her classmates and neighbours. At home she wasn't expected to share in the housework.

Despite her love for her father, Muambule refused to be baptised in his church, and she began to attend Mass and catechism classes at the local Catholic church. She wanted to be baptised but needed her family's permission, which her father withheld. From the age of 10 she wanted to be a nun, but didn't feel called to any of the local communities.

Finally, in May 1972, her father gave in and consented to her baptism, though he refused to give her a special dress for the ceremony or to organise a party. But when Muambule, soon to be Astrid, got up on the morning of her baptism on 3 June, her father had a new dress for her and had arranged a party. On the same day, 7,000 kilometres away in France, a group of Poor Clares were blessed as they set out to found the Monastery of the Holy Trinity in Kabinda.

When she was 14, Astrid's father wanted to arrange a marriage for her, but she resisted for the next four years. During this time she had an experience which marked her for life. She went into the church near the market to pray in front of a large crucifix, which she'd often seen before. In an echo of Francis' experience at St Damiano, it seemed that Jesus himself spoke to her, and she had a new-found desire to imitate Jesus, to help him and to console him in his sufferings.

When she was 18 Astrid heard for the first time of the Poor Clares – 'sisters who never go out and who pray a lot'.[38] This was what she longed for. A few days later she was taken to the Monastery of the Holy Trinity and was soon accepted as an aspirant, and she began to spend one Sunday a month there. Her family were aghast, especially as the community held manual work to be important and her family thought she was unsuited to it. Her former classmates told her she wouldn't last a week, that the sisters would throw her out, but Astrid persevered, and on 18 August 1979 she entered the monastery, becoming a novice a year later, when she took the name of Claire.

From the beginning she loved the life of prayer, but the manual work and community life caused her (and the other sisters) real difficulties. She was no good at housework, cookery or gardening and tried to do as little of them as possible. She couldn't see that they had any spiritual value and wanted to spend all her time in prayer and study. Nor was she good at relationships with others; unless she was the centre of attention, she remained aloof.

The Novice Guardian told Claire, 'It is God himself who has chosen us to live together,'[39] and these words made an impact on Claire, who tried by force of will to participate better. Her sisters, however, could tell her heart wasn't in it, and many of them thought she should leave. But the Abbess supported her, and on 11 August 1982 she made her vows, as Sister Claire of the Eucharist, though she continued to struggle with the communal life and her practical work.

Then in January 1983, a young American woman, Kim Kollins, called to a ministry of healing and conversion, came to speak to local religious communities. She exhorted them to give their lives to God once again and to receive a fresh outpouring of the Spirit. Claire listened intently, and something shifted inside her. She began to weep for her sins and to see the reality of God's love and mercy for her. From now on she let God lead her and work in her, and, although the change wasn't immediate, she was gradually transformed – peaceful and joyous at work and genuinely attentive to others.

This was all the more impressive as she had been in poor health since September 1982, suffering with a blocked nose and head-aches, which made it hard to breathe and to sleep. Initial treatment made no difference, and the local hospital could offer no more. On 11 August 1983 she renewed her vows and had a profound experience of Jesus looking at her and asking, 'Do you want to help me carry the cross?', to which she replied, 'Yes.'[40] She sensed something was happening, and others saw it too. Father Constant, the local Catholic priest, solidly Flemish, came into the chapel and saw her deep in prayer in front of the tabernacle, radiant with light. He believed that he had seen something of the glory of God shining on and around Claire.

In October 1983 Claire went with Sister Hortense to the American hospital, an eight-hour drive on bad roads. A dental X-ray showed a mass in her jaw, which the surgeon believed was probably cancerous, and he operated to remove it. Tests showed that he was right, and Claire was told that she had only three months to live. Through all of this she was calm and often joyful. Before the operation she made her confession and received Communion. Then, as she waited, she asked for the cross to be brought to her and said to Jesus, 'Lord Jesus, I give you my life for priests, and for all who disown you.' Members of the hospital staff began to come to her room to pray with her; outsiders heard of her and came to visit, and she had the right words for all of them.

When she returned home, she was weak, with poor sight and balance, and unable to chew her food. But she continued to join the life of the community as much as possible. Every morning she went to a covered terrace where she prayed and received many visitors. In a total transformation from how she had been, they had her total attention. When a priest asked how she seemed to have the wisdom to address all the questions people brought her, she replied that she was empty, but that she prayed and then waited for the words which the Spirit gave her, and then spoke.

It was agreed that Claire would make her vows for life on Christmas Eve. Initially she didn't see the need, feeling that she had already given her life to God, but in reality the time of preparation was very precious and richly blessed. Late in November, she said, 'Brother Cancer is doing his work, and I'm doing mine.' When asked what her work was, she replied, 'My work is to praise God, to praise him in joy, in suffering, in all that I am!'[41]

Her life profession was a simple and moving service, with her sisters, family, priests and other religious present. In the new year her illness continued to worsen. By the last month of her life she was paralysed and bedbound, 'barely able to see, her face disfigured, able to swallow only liquids, speaking with difficulty, and giving off a nauseating smell'.[42] But her prayer was still full of joy and of life. She said, 'Thank you, Lord, for all you have done! All that you have created is good, even Brother Cancer who is preparing me to come to you! And if he hurries up, so I see you soon, that's fine by me!'[43]

For the last three days of her life she was on the verge of a coma, but made her Communion, and her sisters came to sing the Magnificat for her. At 7.30 pm on 1 April 1984, she gave a loud cry and died. She was 24.

Claire's body was laid on the veranda, and more than 500 people came to pray and to sing until the following afternoon when her funeral took place. Father Constant read these words at the start of the service:

> Very often Sister Claire spoke of this day: the day of her entry into the Kingdom, the day of her Resurrection with Christ. And she asked and insisted that today's event, her death and her burial, be a feast of praise to God; she asked for joy and gratitude. So I say, in the name of Sister Claire, of her community, her family – welcome and thank you!
> Sister Claire is in the glory of the Lord; I invite everyone to celebrate this day with serenity, with joy in meditation and with

great faith and a heart full of gratitude for this admirable life, for the wonders of the Lord, the kindness of her Spouse.[44]

Rather less dramatic were the lives of two of my own community, Gabriel and Ramon. Both ended their lives as hermits; perhaps surprisingly both were extroverts, with many years of active ministry behind them.

Gabriel was born in 1912, and although her family were well-to-do, she insisted on training as a secretary, a skill she used as an officer in the Women's Royal Naval Service during World War II. Those of us who knew her later, as a very determined sister, used to say that if the Nazis had known Gabriel was on our side, they may have decided to surrender sooner. In her mid-40s Gabriel joined CSF, where she turned her hand to anything, though her greatest love was the garden. She also did parish work and then lived in a joint house of brothers and sisters in north Wales, where she used her social skills in hospitality and also learnt to cook. It was here that she began to feel the call to a more solitary life and, after trying it out in various places, settled into a converted cricket pavilion at Compton Durville in Somerset.

She was by now about 70 years old, with poor sight, and so always needed some help. In regular phone calls to the convent she made her requests for the day, everything from a lettuce to make lunch for her spiritual director to someone to fix her kettle, to the name of someone in the news to inform her prayers. Each of us had our particular use, and some mornings a whole queue of us would be taking our turn on the phone to get our instructions. But she took her commitment to a life of prayer very seriously. She stayed in touch with many people, first by letter, then by phone, and was meticulous in praying for them all.

Another sister wrote of her, 'During her last years increasing physical frailty never daunted her from attempting the impossible.'[45] This included the unwise. When we suggested that walking to the convent down the middle of the road might be unsafe, she simply said, 'They'll stop for me,' and, of course, they did. Eventually she became unable to manage alone, even with help, and moved to a community house. Soon after, she died; singular to the end, she was found on her feet at the washbasin in her room, having died suddenly and silently. She was 86 and had been in vows for 37 years.

Ramon had less than 20 years in vows, but made an enormous impact on all he met. Born in Swansea in 1936, he was initially a Welsh Baptist evangelist and pastor, then moved to the Anglican church, where he was ordained, and finally in 1978 became a Franciscan novice. A friend describes him thus:

> His exuberant personality, his uninhibited joy and his breathless energy were infectious. His humour was almost childlike and, wherever he was, there was laughter and fun. He could mimic and tease. He had a fund of stories for every occasion and he shared his life openly and generously with all with whom he came into contact.[46]

His own experience of various churches meant he could open their riches to others. 'Only he could get Anglo-Catholics to sing Elim choruses and a conference of Baptist ministers to handle the rosary.'[47]

Although Ramon seemed to be the last person to embrace a solitary life, he had begun to feel drawn in this direction even before joining the Franciscans. His many gifts were, like Gabriel's, put to full use as a friar – he could range from gardening and habit-making through bookbinding and writing poetry to leading retreats and preaching. Soon after he made vows in 1981 he asked permission to spend six months in solitude in a secluded part of the friary grounds, and this time set the pattern for his future, more permanent life, as a hermit. Following another six months, this time in a remote cottage in north Wales, he moved to the brothers' most contemplative house, Glasshampton, where for seven years he taught novices, wrote books and shared the work of the house.

The call to solitude had not gone away, and in 1990 he began living in a caravan in the grounds of an Anglican convent in south Wales. Life was simple and frugal; as well as caring for his own needs, he undertook some practical work for the sisters. But at the heart of every day was time spent in prayer, interceding for people for whom he'd promised to pray, meditating and on Sundays celebrating the Eucharist in his caravan. He met a very small number of people to share their spiritual journey and kept up correspondence with others. In 1993, following some health concerns, he moved back to Glasshampton, where he could live in three huts near the monastery. Though simple, they were less ascetic than the caravan and were deemed better for his health. One was his living quarters, another his chapel and the third a workshop where he could make prayer stools and sandals, mount icons and bind books. He had a steady stream of visitors seeking his spiritual advice and counsel, and he continued to write many letters. In 1998 he was diagnosed with cancer, which was treated with radiotherapy. As he became weaker he moved back into the monastery itself, but not before collaborating with Simon Barrington-Ward on his final book, on the Jesus Prayer. Ramon died in June 2000, aged 64.

Through their different lives, both of these present-day Franciscans witness to the irresistible call of God, leading by surprising paths to unexpected ways of living. Both found joy and contentment in their solitary lives of prayer; both had to accept giving them up as older age and ill health made it necessary; both remained sure that God was still guiding them.

For reflection

- Darleen Pryds writes that Angela of Foligno 'could be brutally honest in revealing her inner struggle that emerged with her religious conversion'.[48] How honest are you able to be, with yourself, with God, with others? Can you also enable others to express their own struggles on their spiritual journey, without feeling the need to make everything more acceptable?

- Jacopone da Todi wrote his 'lauds' in his own language, not the official Latin of the church. What is your 'native tongue' in speaking to God? It may be words, silence, movement or music, or something else entirely. Have you ever felt that you needed to change your 'language' to be acceptable or to fit in? How can you become freer in speaking to and of God?

- Veronica Giuliani sought to become a 'true image' of Christ. Might you be willing to pray that you would also follow this path and go where it leads? This is not to be undertaken lightly, and it would be wise to seek experienced advice and support.

- What might you learn from Claire of the Eucharist about the role of suffering in your relationship with God? Reflect on a time of suffering, whether physical, emotional or spiritual. How did it affect your relationship with God then and, looking back now, do you see anything differently? Take your reflections into prayer.

- Do you naturally draw on your feelings in your spiritual life, happy to express them to God and to speak of them to at least some others? Or are you reluctant to believe that what you feel is real? How might some of the very passionately feeling people in this chapter help you to see and experience this as a legitimate dimension of the life of faith?

5

REFLECTING THE LOVE OF CHRIST: SOCIAL CARE, SOCIAL JUSTICE

From the intense and often enclosed world of the mystics we move out to those who expressed their love of Christ in service of his world. Some were hands-on in this caring; others used their resources and influence to found and support hospitals and other caring institutions. Where those in the previous chapter were often friars or Poor Clares, these often belonged to the Third Order (see chapter 1). And the first people we will meet are traditionally believed to have been the very first members of the Third Order.

Luchesio and Buonadonna were a married couple living in the time of Francis. Luchesio was born around 1180 and, after serving as a soldier, he settled between Florence and Siena. He married Buonadonna and became a merchant. Poggibonsi, where they lived, was on a pilgrim route to Rome, and they sold provisions to the pilgrims. Sadly their reputation was not good; they were greedy and unfeeling, determined to make the maximum profit for themselves.

But in his 30s, Luchesio had a conversion experience and began to change his life. His wife followed suit, and together they started to serve the poor of their area, sharing their wealth. As often happened at the time, they considered separating and entering religious orders to devote themselves to God. When in 1213 Francis visited

Poggibonsi, they asked his advice, and he suggested they remain a married couple and continue their life of service and penitence where they were. They agreed and thus became two of the first, if not the first, members of the Brothers and Sisters of Penance, received as members by Francis himself.

They were faithful to the decision they had made, keeping only a small piece of farmland for themselves and using all their resources to help the poor and needy. And their relationship with one another was strong to the end. When Buonadonna saw her now 80-year-old husband failing, she begged him not to die before her. They died on the same day, 28 April 1260. They had set a pattern for tertiaries of combining family life with prayer and service wherever they lived. God could be served without entering a monastery or convent.

Next we move to a dynasty – a royal network of kings and queens, influenced by Francis and the Franciscans. The first is **Elizabeth of Hungary**, born in 1207. The daughter of King Andrew II, she was sent, aged four, to Thuringia in Germany, the court of her future husband, Ludwig. Thuringia was close to Eisenach, where Franciscan brothers arrived in the early 1220s, and she was strongly influenced by them to a life of prayer and service of the poor. She was generous in giving alms, selling her jewels and costly dresses and giving away the proceeds. She also gave her time and energy, personally visiting and nursing the sick.

Her husband was supportive of her, but he died in 1227, by which time they already had four children. The following year Elizabeth made a public commitment to poverty. Her spiritual director, Conrad of Marburg, wrote:

> On Good Friday... after the altars had been stripped, she knelt in front of the altar of the chapel she had given to the Friars Minor and laid her hands on it. Then in their presence she renounced her own will, her earthly estate and all that our Saviour counsels us in the gospel to put aside.[49]

Elizabeth established a hospital in Marburg and worked there until her death, aged 24. She was canonised four years later and is now honoured as one of the patrons of the Third Order, though it isn't clear whether she was ever officially a member. Either way, her life certainly reflected their values.

The other official patron of the Third Order is **Louis of France**, a contemporary of Elizabeth. Again there is no historical record that he actually joined the tertiaries, but his values were undoubtedly those of the order. Born in 1214, he long outlived Elizabeth, dying in 1270. Louis was the son of Philip II and became king of France at the age of 12, though he wasn't crowned until he was 21. His mother, Blanche of Castile, was very devout and raised him strictly, with a strong sense of responsibility.

A famous illuminated manuscript of the 14th century contains a set of pictures of Louis' life. The manuscript belonged to his great-great-granddaughter, Jeanne de Navarre, who therefore had a special connection with the saint, and at the time the book was made, 60 years after his death, there may just have been people alive who had known him. The pictures include one of him learning to read and another of him attending Mass. Christopher de Hamel imagines Jeanne de Navarre using the book to teach her own children to read, introducing them to their illustrious and saintly ancestor at the same time.[50]

Louis was seen even in his own day as a model Christian ruler, seeking to keep peace and make justice available to all. He outlawed usury, the excessive rates of interest that were ruining many people, had poor people fed at his table and was very supportive of both Franciscans and Dominicans. During a pilgrimage he went to Perugia to visit Giles, one of Francis' companions (see chapter 8). He arrived unannounced and asked for Giles without saying who he was. But Giles, through the Spirit, knew who he was; he left his cell and ran to meet Louis. They embraced warmly and then sat together in silence, before Louis continued his journey. When the other brothers questioned Giles about why they had not spoken, he said that divine wisdom had revealed their hearts to one another, and speech was unnecessary.

Louis had a strong sense of being 'God's lieutenant', and this led to him joining the Seventh Crusade, from 1248 to 1254, during which he was captured. It's possible that it was during this time that he acquired the elephant which he sent as a gift to Henry III of England in 1255. It caused a sensation when it arrived, but it was an expensive gift to receive. Special accommodation had to be built at the Tower of London for the elephant, and a keeper paid to care for it. Sadly the elephant died two years later. In 1270 Louis himself launched the Eighth Crusade, but died of dysentery in Tunis on the way to the eastern Mediterranean.

Another royal Elizabeth is **Isabel of Portugal** (1271–1336), a great-niece of Elizabeth of Hungary, after whom she was named. At age 11, she was married to King Denis of Portugal, who was a good king but an unfaithful husband. Isabel bore with this patiently, being faithful in prayer and generous to the poor. She endowed hospitals and other religious projects.

More unusually, she was also active politically and became known as 'the peacemaker'; she mediated in a dispute between her husband and the king of Castile and in 1297 brought about a treaty which fixed the boundary between Portugal and Spain. Later she intervened in a civil war between her husband and their son Alfonso, heir to the throne. When words failed to bring them together, she rode out on to the battlefield on a donkey, shaming them into reconciliation. As Denis became older, he repented of his earlier ways and praised his wife's wisdom. In a poem to her he wrote:

Seeing as God made you without peer
In goodness of heart and goodness of speech,
Nor is your equal anywhere to be found,
My love, my lady, I hereby tell you:

Had God desired to ordain it so,
You would have made a great king.[51]

Denis died in 1325, and Isabel joined the Third Order, living next to the Poor Clare monastery in Coimbra, which she had refounded. Like her great-aunt, she gave up most of her possessions and endowed a hospital there. She also continued to be a peacemaker – aged over 60 she travelled to broker a peace agreement between her son, now King of Portugal, and her son-in-law the king of Castile. But the effort wore her out and she died on 4 July 1336.

Her peacemaking efforts were echoed by my brothers in the Solomon Islands, during a time of internal conflict and ethnic tension between 1999 and 2000. In an effort to bring warring groups together, some of them went out and camped in the land between them, continuing their life of prayer and service and inviting those from both sides to join them in daily prayer. It was a bold intervention, which did indeed help to bring reconciliation. They were lucky to all come back to their friaries alive and well; another religious community, the Melanesian Brotherhood, who also mediated in the conflict, had seven members kidnapped and killed in 2003 as they sought to persuade a former rebel leader to respect the peace agreement. They are now honoured as martyrs, and some of our brothers were present in Canterbury Cathedral when their sacrifice was recognised.[52]

Our next royal is another Louis, **Louis of Toulouse**, a great nephew of both Elizabeth of Hungary and Louis of France and a contemporary of Isabel of Portugal. Born in 1274, he was the son of Charles II, king of Naples. His father inherited the throne in 1285 but was at the time a prisoner of the king of Aragon; several years later he was freed but had to send three of his sons, including Louis, as hostages to Barcelona. Louis was 14 at the time and spent seven years there, educated by the Friars Minor. When released, he renounced his royal status and entered the Order in 1296. Obviously his Franciscan teachers had done a good job.

Pope Boniface VIII didn't think a prince should be an ordinary friar and named Louis bishop of Toulouse. Determined to live as a poor Franciscan, Louis gave half of the revenues of his diocese to the poor and fed 25 poor people every day at his own table. He kept repeating, 'Jesus Christ is all my riches; he alone is sufficient for me,' consciously or unconsciously echoing Francis' words in 'The Praises of God'.

Louis died suddenly in 1297, before he could renounce his bishopric, and was canonised in 1317, the third Friar Minor to be declared a saint (Francis himself and Anthony of Padua being the first two). It's interesting to speculate on the impact which Louis could have had if he had lived longer, but he crammed much into a short life.

Our final royal is **Ferdinand of Castile**, and with him we return to the early days of Franciscan influence and to the Third Order. Born in 1201, he was a successful king of Castile and Leon, taking the cities of Cordoba and Seville from their Arab rulers. But he also had a strong sense of justice, especially in his laws and taxes, with a care for the poor. He said that he 'feared the curses of one poor woman more than an army of Saracens'. He died in 1252 and was buried in his Third Order habit. The multicultural reality of his kingdom was reflected in the inscription on his tomb, which was in Latin, Arabic, Hebrew and Castilian.

Margaret of Cortona came from a much less illustrious background, and some parts of her story wouldn't be out of place in a tabloid. Born into an Italian farming family in 1247, Margaret's mother died when she was young, and she didn't get on with her stepmother. When she was 18 she ran away from home and began work for a nobleman, with whom she started a relationship and had a son. They never married, perhaps because of their very different social status, but lived together as husband and wife. One day, when she was 27, her lover's dog returned alone to the castle; she followed the dog and found her partner's body. He had been attacked by robbers and left to die in a ditch.

To the shock of her bereavement was added the fact that she had no rights to inherit anything and had to leave the castle with her son. Her family refused to take her back, so she was left with nothing. She settled in the town of Cortona, where two devout noblewomen helped them to begin a new life. Margaret began to work as a midwife to support herself and her son, and she also began to grow in faith.

In 1277 she joined the Third Order, though the friars were reluctant to receive her because of her chequered past. Unconvinced of her conversion, they thought she might return to a life of sin and cause scandal. But she proved them wrong and for the rest of her life combined active service and contemplation. Her role as a midwife developed into a wider care for the sick, poor and homeless. With the help of the noblewomen of Cortona she founded a hospital, and eventually a group of women helped her in this work.

More controversially she apparently baptised many of the babies she delivered. Although lay baptism had been not uncommon, by this time baptising was becoming a priestly role and there was pressure on her to give it up. It's speculation, but perhaps she was especially in demand by those women who had children from irregular relationships, who came to her knowing they would receive understanding and support, rather than condemnation. We know of this activity only by a reference, in the life written by her confessor, to Margaret giving up this ministry because it was taking up too much of her time – a clear indication that it was not just the occasional emergency baptism of a seriously ill newborn. It seems that women were seeking her out to baptise their babies.

Margaret was much in demand as a spiritual guide to the local friars and other people of Cortona, as well as those throughout Italy and as far away as Spain. She also acted as a mediator between the bishop and the people of the city, continuing the Franciscan work of peacemaking. Towards the end of her life she committed herself more and more to prayer, living as a solitary, though still available to give spiritual guidance. She died in 1297 and was immediately venerated by the people of Cortona as a saint, though not officially canonised until 1728.

Angela Merici is another Italian woman whose life included membership of the Third Order. Her particular passion was for the education of girls and young women. Born in 1474 and orphaned at an early age, she began her ministry by teaching in her own home and joined the Third Order as an expression of her desire to live a celibate life of service to others.

The city of Brescia invited her to move there and set up a school, and she also began organising groups of unmarried women for mutual support. In 1535 twelve other women formally joined her in what they called the 'Company of St Ursula' after the medieval patron saint of education. Angela did not want to found a religious community in the accepted sense of the day. The women of the company did not wear a habit and lived a celibate life in their own homes. They met regularly for prayer and spiritual conferences. In many ways she anticipated some very recent developments in forms of religious life, often described as 'new monasticism'. Angela died in 1540, only five years after the founding of her company, but they had already spread to 24 cities. She had obviously started something which many women wanted to be part of.

Angela was buried as a Franciscan tertiary, but in the decades after her death the Company of St Ursula became a formal religious order, the Ursulines, who see Angela as their founder. In the small Rule she wrote for her companions, Angela asked them to obey 'the counsels and inspirations which the Holy Spirit unceasingly sends into our hearts'.[53] She certainly seems to have followed this herself.

Another woman honoured as a founder is **Mary Frances Schervier**. Unlike Margaret of Cortona and Angela Merici, whose lives were bounded by Italy, she oversaw a community which from its beginnings in Germany soon went to America also to fulfil its Franciscan calling. Mary Frances herself visited the USA twice; on the first occasion, in 1863, she helped her sisters in nursing casualties of the American Civil War.

Born Franziska Schervier to a wealthy family in Aachen, Germany, in 1819, from the age of 13 she had to manage the household after the death of her mother. The Industrial Revolution had begun, and many poor people were living in terrible conditions. Franziska began to nurse them in their own homes and helped in a soup kitchen, despite opposition from her father. After her father died, Franziska became a member of the Third Order and by 1845 had gathered together a group of women to form a community dedicated to service of the poor. Franziska became Mary Frances and the superior of this small new group, officially recognised by the church in 1851 as the Poor Sisters of St Francis.

Their work expanded to include the care of prostitutes and those suffering from syphilis, work which caused some benefactors to withdraw their support. As they depended entirely on charity, this meant they lived in extreme poverty. But they were not deterred; new members came, and by the late 1850s they had also sent sisters to America, to minister to German migrants there. In both America and Europe, they founded hospitals for those suffering from tuberculosis. It seems to have been one of Mary Frances' strong points to see the needs of her day and to act. She did not stop with her initial vision, but continued to develop it. When she died in 1876, there were 2,500 members of her community worldwide.

Francis' ministry to lepers is often used as a touchstone by Franciscans, who ask, 'Who are today's lepers?' For Mary Frances it included prostitutes; for some of my own brothers and sisters, the answer has been those living and dying with HIV/AIDS, refugees and asylum seekers.

In America **Ruth**, one of the sisters in San Francisco, realised there was a need for somewhere for relatives of those dying of AIDS in local hospitals to stay. Many came from a long way away, and reaching

San Francisco exhausted their financial resources. In addition, for a lot of them, the terminal diagnosis was a total shock; they had not known that their son or brother was infected or at risk. So Ruth, with the help of local friends, founded the Family Link, providing accommodation and pastoral support for these people. The project continues today, though with a much wider remit, as AIDS has become a chronic and not a terminal condition.

In the UK, a sister, trained as a nurse, worked with people being tested for the virus, and a number of brothers supported the sick and the dying. Houses offered hospitality and support to visiting relatives. At a time when there was great concern about the virus being easily transmitted, and when funeral directors sometimes refused to organise funerals, **Colin Wilfred** in particular would lay out the bodies of those who had died and take their funerals, once taking 14 in one week. For ten years, in the UK and New York, he offered pastoral support, but he also spoke out:

> 'The church has AIDS', he used to say often. He campaigned, he cried, he wrote, he preached, he lobbied, he led pilgrimages to Lourdes, he laughed, he did liturgy, and, of course, he arranged the furniture.[54]

That last comment is a reminder that we are all more than our ministry; Colin had an eye for order and beauty and couldn't be in a room without improving how it looked, moving the furniture and adding a liturgical focal point. He was also completely technophobic and only had to look at a photocopier or fax machine for it to break.

The needs of the world move on, and now my brothers in several parts of the UK are involved in working with refugees and asylum seekers, in particular offering accommodation to those whose applications have been refused and who are therefore cut off from any financial support. They work with them to submit appeals, which are often successful, and then help them to move on to make a new life. Some also teach English, helping the newcomers to integrate.

John Bradburne was another, like Mary Frances Schervier, whose desire to reflect the love of Christ in care for others led him to travel widely. Born in 1921 in Cumbria, England, he was the son of an Anglican clergyman. He joined the army in 1939 and fought with the Gurkhas in Malaya and Burma. In Malaya, some kind of religious experience began his pilgrimage of faith, and in 1947, back in England, he became a Roman Catholic. He wanted to become a monk and spent time with various communities, but didn't settle with any of them. Instead, he spent the next 16 years travelling around France, Italy, Greece and the Middle East. He took odd jobs, such as teaching, caretaking and forestry, but didn't settle to anything. He had a very good voice and wrote large amounts of poetry; sometimes he called himself a troubadour, a description which also fits Francis. At some stage in all of this John joined the Third Order.

In 1962 he felt the urge to settle and wrote to a man he had known in the Gurkhas who was now a Jesuit priest in Rhodesia, now Zimbabwe, asking, 'Is there a cave in Africa where I can pray?' Soon after his arrival he confided three wishes to a Franciscan priest: he wanted to serve leprosy patients, to die a martyr and to be buried in the habit of St Francis. In 1969 the first of his wishes was fulfilled when he was appointed warden at Mutemwa Leprosy Settlement, about 90 miles east of Salisbury, now Harare. There were around 80 lepers there, living in dreadful conditions, often hungry and in huts that were falling down. John Bradburne had found what he wanted and never left.

He cared tenderly for the lepers, cutting the nails of those who still had fingers and toes, sitting with the dying, building a small church and teaching them music for the services. But the Leprosy Association, which ran Mutemwa, was unhappy with his work. They wanted the lepers to be known only by numbered tags around their necks, whereas he gave each one a name and an individual poem. They thought he was extravagant because he insisted each leper had at least one loaf of bread a week. In 1973, the Leprosy Association sacked him from his job and he had to leave. However, he didn't go far, but found a small prefab hut just outside the settlement and continued to serve the lepers as much as he could.

For the rest of the time he prayed and wrote poetry, living very simply. When the Zimbabwean civil war broke out he was advised to leave, but refused to do so and stayed on to protect the leprosy patients. In September 1979 he was abducted by guerrillas; when they tried to interrogate him, he said little, but knelt and prayed. They had local information that he was harmless, but feared he now knew too much about them. On 5 September he was shot and his body left by the roadside.

At his funeral, a small pool of blood formed underneath his coffin. When the coffin was opened, there was no sign of blood, but it was seen that he had not been buried in his Third Order habit, as he had hoped to be. The habit was then put on his body and the coffin closed up again. This was just the first of a number of unexplained events, including healings, which have made Mutemwa, still a leper settlement, a place of pilgrimage and have led to the formation of a society that has published a selection of his poetry and continues to support the settlement. Their work to have John Bradburne considered for canonisation as a saint is bearing fruit: on the 40th anniversary of his death the Vatican formally started the process of investigation.[55]

Whatever we make of his story, John Bradburne is a striking recent example of someone whose desire to know God and to care for those most in need led him to an extraordinary life. There are undoubtedly many more like him, whose names and stories are not widely known, but whose lives and service are no less extraordinary.

One of my own sisters also travelled widely to serve God's people, though her story has a happier ending than that of John Bradburne. **Leonore** was born in 1909, the daughter of an army officer. After a brief attempt at teaching, she pursued what had always been her other career choice – medicine. She studied in Edinburgh and qualified in surgery at a time when this was very unusual for a woman. She had a flair for languages and wanted to serve abroad, so after qualification she went to India, to the Christian Medical College at Ludhiana, eventually becoming Professor of Anatomy.

During a furlough at home in 1954 she joined the Third Order, but when two years later she felt she had to test her vocation to the religious life, she chose to join a community which enabled her to stay in India – the Oxford Mission Sisters of the Epiphany, based in Barisal. She made her profession with them in January 1961 and worked as a doctor, surgeon and midwife, as well as training nurses and, as she recalled in her memoirs, making mosquito nets for cows. All this went alongside the daily round of religious life with her sisters, and with the parallel community of brothers who lived alongside them.

When the Pakistan-Bangladesh war broke out in 1971 the communities came under threat, and after one attack it was Leonore, going round the compound, who found the brother's superior, Father Macbeth, dead at his desk. He had been knifed in the back. She also had to help the community cope with floods, food shortages and rebuilding works.

In the 1970s Leonore's health began to be seriously affected by the Indian conditions, and it was decided she must return to the UK. But her community had no house here. She had stayed with CSF after a hip operation in the early 1970s and asked to come to us again, with a view to transfer. Finally, in March 1978, this took place, and at the age of 69 Leonore officially became a member of CSF.

She was unable to practise medicine in the UK, as she was well over retirement age and out of touch with modern medical practice. But she moved to a new Franciscan house in the East End of London, where her ability to speak Bengali and her medical knowledge were put to good use at the London Hospital, interpreting especially for Bengali women and in the Well Babies' Clinic. This work earned her an MBE in 1985. She was very happy there. She was less happy when she had to move back to Somerset, and somewhat frustrated at times. I remember her being the ideal person to ask to carve the Christmas turkey – her surgical skills were put to full use. She also made habits, but this was rather less successful, and after one sister was given a habit with the sleeves put in backwards, it was agreed that perhaps this was not her forte. Towards the end of her life she asked to move to a nursing home, where she died in July 1997.

Finally, an organisation, not an individual. **Franciscans International** (FI) was founded in 1989 as a non-profit, international human rights organisation. It has offices in Geneva and New York, from which staff work to bring the lived experience of the poorest in the world to the attention of those who have the power to address injustice through structural change. It is an initiative of the Franciscan family, including the Anglican Franciscans, and the governing body reflects this ecumenical status.

FI describes its mission as being 'a Franciscan voice at the United Nations protecting the vulnerable, the forgotten, and the wounded earth through advocacy'.[56] Many of its campaigns are sparked by the work of Franciscans of all three orders working throughout the world. For example, in Benin, they have been working with Franciscans in the country since 2011 to end the infanticide of children who, because of a disability or premature or breech birth, are believed to bring bad luck to the family and are therefore killed or abandoned. In 2015, following pressure by repeated UN recommendations, the Benin government adopted a new code criminalising ritual infanticide.

In the Philippines, a group of Franciscan sisters developed strong links and trusted relationships with indigenous leaders, concerned at the operation of illegal black sand mining. This affects coastal communities, depleting fisheries, worsening flooding and causing salt water and chemicals to pollute the fresh water needed to grow rice. FI was able to use the sisters' expertise and contacts to campaign at the UN for an end to this mining and also to mobilise the local community to campaign on the ground. In 2014 the mining was banned, and the mining companies were forced to rehabilitate the area they had damaged. The local communities, emboldened by this victory and enabled by the training and support they have received, are monitoring to ensure no further damaging mining takes place.

In a globalised world, FI is an example of how the experience of Franciscans and others on the ground can make a difference. It would have amazed many of our previous followers of Francis to see this work and to know that their successors in working for social care and social justice have the ability to speak to the nations of the world. The love of Christ can now be reflected much more powerfully and the voice of the poor and powerless amplified so that the powerful can hear.

For reflection

- Although the early Franciscans were 'Lesser Brothers' and 'Poor Clares', they soon found themselves working with and ministering to the powerful as well as those in need. Who are the royalty of today? You might think of governments, large multinational companies, international entertainers. How might we as Christians influence them? And what does the example of Franciscans International have to teach us?

- Members of the Third Order have always been called to combine their family and working life with a commitment to prayer and ministry. What might their pattern of life have to offer to all those Christians seeking to hold together these dimensions of life? If this is your life, how does it work for you, and where do you struggle?

- Margaret of Cortona found it hard to change her life because people did not believe she really wanted to. Do we judge people only by their past, or do we believe in the possibility of conversion and redemption? Has this been a problem for you or for someone you know? Pray for open minds and hearts in the church and the world.

- When might it be right to break church rules for the sake of ministry? What do the examples of Margaret of Cortona and John Bradburne have to teach us? Do you have any experience of this in your own life? How did or do you feel about it? Would you do it again?

6

THE WAY OF RENUNCIATION AND SACRIFICE: MARTYRS

Many of the church's earliest saints were martyrs. Along with the reality of Christianity being a persecuted faith went a desire to follow Christ in a very literal way. He had laid down his life, to the point of death; those who followed him could expect to do nothing less. In fact, the word 'martyr' means 'witness', and the early martyrs were those who witnessed in life and in death to the supreme importance of their faith.

Franciscan martyrs are in this mould. Their stories can be painful to read and their examples hard to follow. Most of us are not called to missionary work in dangerous places, which was often the context of martyrdom. But, of course, we're all aware of the many Christians whose faith does put them in grave danger today. So perhaps we read these stories as a way of reminding ourselves that this is part of our heritage of faith and in order to ask ourselves, 'What is important enough for me that I would give my life for it?'

Many of the martyrs come in groups, which makes their witness more impressive but can make it harder to relate to them. The first Franciscan martyrs are like this; they died in 1220, while Francis was still alive. In 1219 Francis sent brothers to various places in Europe – France, Germany, Hungary and Spain – to preach the gospel. Those who went to Germany didn't speak the language; the only word they knew was 'Ja' (yes). This was fine so long as they were being asked if they wanted shelter or food. It was disastrous when they were being asked whether they were heretics. Answering 'yes' to that got them beaten up or thrown into prison. However, they did all return safely to Italy.

Five of those who went to southern Spain, then a Muslim territory, also had little success and went on to Morocco instead. The leader of the group was **Berard**, and his companions were **Peter**, **Otto**, **Accursius** and **Adjutus**. Evangelising openly was seen as blasphemy against Islam, and local Christians and civil authorities tried to dissuade the friars from preaching in public. However they continued to do so and were executed by beheading on 16 January 1220.

'The blood of the martyrs is the seed of the church,' said Tertullian in the early church, and here we see a vivid example of that reality. When the bodies of the martyrs were brought to Coimbra in Portugal, where the Franciscans had a small hermitage, their sacrifice so impressed a young Augustinian canon that he decided to join the Franciscans instead. That young man was Anthony of Padua, one of the great preachers of the Franciscan family.

These first martyrs died because of enmity between faiths; our next group died because of enmity within the Christian church. They were executed in Ireland in the 16th and 17th centuries for the 'crime' of being Catholics. Following Henry VIII's conquest of Ireland in 1536, he sought to make it a Protestant country, and the Penal Laws came into force to make it much harder to be Catholic. Catholic priests were usually tolerated, but bishops had to operate clandestinely; services had to take place in private. This was the setting for these Franciscan martyrs.

Patrick O'Healey, born around 1543, became a Franciscan as a young man and trained for the priesthood in Spain, where he also taught. He was appointed bishop of Mayo in 1576. When he eventually reached Ireland, along with a priest, **Conn O'Rourke**, they were soon betrayed. Functioning as a Catholic bishop was treason, and Patrick was tortured and hanged in 1579, along with Conn.

Conor O'Devaney, born around 1532, also joined the Franciscans as a young man and studied and ministered on continental Europe. At around the age of 50, he was appointed bishop of Down and Connor, and back in Ireland was arrested in 1588 during the anti-Catholic panic that followed the Spanish Armada. Protected by the powerful O'Neill family, he was released and continued as a bishop. In 1611 he was arrested again, and this time he was found guilty of treason and hanged in Dublin. His story shows something of the unpredictability of dangerous times and of the interplay of faith and politics that often determines the outcome, for good or for ill.

The last of our representative Irish martyrs is **John Kearney**, born in 1619, who studied in Leuven in Belgium and was ordained in Brussels in 1642. He returned to Ireland and was much admired for his preaching. During Oliver Cromwell's campaign in Ireland, however, he was arrested for the crime of ministering as a priest and was hanged in 1653.

Ireland, of course, was not alone in making martyrs of those who belonged to the 'wrong' part of the Christian church. In England **Thomas More** is remembered as a martyr, one who became fatally entangled in the complexities of faith and politics of the early years of the Reformation. Born in 1478, Thomas More was the son of a prosperous lawyer and became a lawyer himself in 1502, the year in which he married. He had contemplated becoming a monk, but decided he would serve God better as a Christian layman. He became a member of the Franciscan Third Order around 1498.

In 1504 he entered Parliament, where he was highly thought of for his eloquence and integrity. Steadily he moved closer to the centre of power, becoming a member of the Privy Council in 1514 and finally Lord Chancellor in 1529. He was a close friend and advisor of Henry VIII and helped the king to write a defence of the Catholic doctrine of the sacraments against the teaching of Luther. But as the king, seeking a divorce from Anne Boleyn, moved to separate the church in England from the authority of the Pope in Rome, More could no longer support him and resigned as Chancellor in 1532. He tried to avoid taking a public position on the king's marriage but found it impossible; his public profile was too high. Arrested in 1534 for denying the new doctrine of the king's supremacy over the church in England, he was executed in 1535.

Another casualty of the Reformation was **Fidelis of Sigmaringen**, born Mark Roy in 1577 in the German town after which he is named. He became a lawyer in Alsace and was known as 'the poor person's lawyer' because of his willingness to work for the poor. In 1612, he became a Franciscan friar and ministered in Austria, where he was valued for his preaching and as a confessor. In 1621 the Vatican asked for priests to go to the Swiss canton of Graubünden, where Calvinism was making major inroads on the Catholic faith of the people. Fidelis, along with several other friars, volunteered for the task of preaching and seeking to commend the Catholic faith to the people. It was a dangerous mission: militant Protestants threatened him, and he often had to be protected by Austrian troops. In spring 1622, while preaching to Catholics at Seewis, exhorting them to remain faithful, a Calvinist shot at him in church. After leaving the church, he was met by a group of Calvinist soldiers, who called him a false prophet and urged him to convert to their faith. He refused and was killed.

The memory of these deaths (and, of course, of many Protestants too) is a spur to reconciliation in today's church. Indeed Pope Francis and Bishop Mounib Younan, president of the Lutheran World Federation, in a joint declaration marking the 500th anniversary of the Reformation, made just this point:

> Our common faith in Jesus Christ and our baptism demand of us a daily conversion, by which we cast off the historical disagreements and conflicts that impede the ministry of reconciliation. While the past cannot be changed, what is remembered and how it is remembered can be transformed... Today, we hear God's command to set aside all conflict. We

recognise that we are freed by grace to move towards the communion to which God continually calls us.[57]

Our next group of martyrs are from around the same time as these Reformation martyrs, but on the other side of the world. In Japan, in 1597, a group of three Jesuits and 23 Franciscans were crucified in Nagasaki. The Jesuits had been the first to arrive – Francis Xavier came in 1549, and he and his brothers tried to reach the more educated Japanese and to express the gospel message in a way which Japanese culture could hear. The Franciscans arrived in 1593 and by contrast began working with lepers and other people on the margins and at the bottom of society. The Franciscans who died were a very mixed group – four Spanish friars, one from Mexico and one from India and 17 Japanese Third Order members, including two young boys, one of whom was only 12.

Once again this horrific violence did not discourage people from becoming Christians. In 1597 there were about 250,000 Christians in Japan; by 1614 there were about 400,000. However, in that year an anti-Christian edict came into force, launching a campaign of torture and slow death to compel people to give up their faith. Shūsaku Endō's 1966 novel, *Silence*, is set in this period. The persecution lasted for 25 years, and only a few Christians remained, who went underground for the next two centuries.

It's easy to ask, 'What was the point?', and it's a hard question to answer. The sacrifice of the Franciscan and Jesuit martyrs, and of many Japanese Christians, seems to have been for nothing. In Japan today there are no prohibitions on being Christian, but the church is very small, with only about 1% of the population identifying as Christian. It's difficult to see in this story any fulfilment of Jesus' promise that 'unless a grain of wheat falls to the ground and dies, it remains only a single seed. But if it dies, it produces many seeds' (John 12:24). Maybe we can only use it to learn to live with the mystery of apparent failure. There is, however, perhaps one small ray of light: a 1996 survey of religious affiliation across the prefectures of Japan found that Nagasaki, where these martyrs died, had the highest proportion of Christians, at 5.1%.[58] Perhaps some of those grains of wheat are still bearing fruit.

Some 300 years later, another group of Franciscans were martyred in the Far East, this time in China. Again they became caught up in political conflict as much as in religious disagreement. In 1898, several European governments insisted on significant concessions from the Chinese empire, both financial and territorial. The Chinese reaction was the Boxer Rebellion, fighting against all foreign influence.

Franciscan friars had been in Shanxi Province for more than 30 years, running a seminary to train Chinese clergy. In 1899 a group of seven sisters arrived, members of the **Franciscan Missionaries of Mary**, to staff an orphanage. They were young women – ranging from 25 to 36 years old – from several European countries. In June the following year, when the situation became very tense, the bishops, fearing for their safety, begged the sisters to put on Chinese clothes and try to save themselves. But they replied, 'For the love of God do not prevent us from dying with you. If our courage is weak, believe me that God who sends the test will give us strength to meet it bravely. We fear neither death nor torments. We came here to exercise charity and to shed our blood for the love of Jesus Christ if need be.'[59]

Early in July 1900 Boxers raided the mission. They captured five friars, all seven sisters, five Chinese seminarians and nine Chinese laypeople employed by the mission, most of whom were Third Order members. The entire group was brutally executed several days later. Protestant missionaries and their families were also targeted and a number were killed, as were over 2,000 Chinese Christians. Here the story ends differently to the Japanese one: 25 years later several hundred Franciscan missionaries were working in China.

Our remaining martyrs are more recent, and individuals, which means there is more material available, and perhaps it's easier to relate to them.

Two died in World War II, victims of the Nazi regime. **Maximilian Kolbe** is the better known of the two. He was born in 1894 near Lodz, in what was then part of the Russian empire, and at the age of 12 had a vision of the virgin Mary, holding out two crowns, one white and one red. The white signified purity and the red martyrdom, and Mary asked if he was willing to accept either. He replied that he was willing to accept both. He was so determined to become a Franciscan that he made the illegal border crossing into the Austro-Hungarian Empire and at the age of 16 became a friar.

Maximilian was highly intelligent, and after making his vows he was sent to Rome, where he obtained two doctorates, in theology and philosophy. In 1919 he returned to Poland, newly independent, where he taught at a seminary and began to publish a monthly magazine, which became very popular, as well as operating a religious publishing house. From 1930 to 1936 Maximilian undertook missionary work, first in Shanghai, where his work was unsuccessful, then in Japan, where he founded a monastery on the outskirts of Nagasaki, which still survives. Poor health forced him to return to Poland, and in 1938 he started a radio station.

When the Germans invaded Poland in 1939, only a few friars remained in the monastery, which provided shelter to refugees, including Jews, and housed a temporary hospital. In February 1941 the monastery was shut down by the authorities, and Kolbe and four others were arrested by the Gestapo and imprisoned. At the end of May Maximilian was transferred to Auschwitz, as prisoner 16670. Throughout this time he continued to act as a priest, which led to harassment by the authorities, including beatings.

At the end of July, three prisoners disappeared from the camp, and in retaliation the deputy camp commander selected ten prisoners at random to be starved to death in an underground bunker. One of these, Franciszek Gajowniczek, cried out, 'My wife! My children!' Moved by pity, Maximilian volunteered to take his place.

During the two weeks which followed, when the prisoners were given neither food nor water, Maximilian Kolbe remained calm, leading them in prayer. One by one the men died; when only Maximilian was left, he was given a lethal injection of carbolic acid and died on 14 August 1941. Having led a very active life, during which he was often in charge of projects and institutions, at the end he was entirely helpless and could only wait for death. It's a sign of the depth of his faith that he was able to do this with grace and still thinking of others.

On Ash Wednesday of the following year, another Franciscan was arrested by the Nazis. **Maria Restituta** was born in the same year as Maximilian Kolbe, 1894, in Austria. She was baptised Helena, trained as a nurse and aged 19 began work at Lainz City Hospital, where she first met the Franciscan Sisters of Christian Charity. Soon she had joined them, making vows in 1915 and life vows a year later. She continued to work as a nurse. When the Austrian Nazi Party took control of the country in 1938, she was outspoken in her opposition to the new regime. When a new wing was built at the hospital at which she worked, she hung a crucifix in each of the new rooms. The Nazi authorities demanded that she remove them, but she refused. Her community said they could not replace her (she was by now lead surgical nurse), and so for several years she continued both her work and her criticism.

In 1942 she was denounced by a doctor who strongly supported the Nazis and arrested as she came out of the operating theatre. The charges against her included hanging crucifixes and writing a poem that mocked Hitler. Brought to court she was found guilty on 29 October of 'favouring the enemy and conspiracy to commit high treason' and sentenced to death by guillotine. She was offered her freedom if she abandoned her membership of her community, but she refused.

Maria remained in prison until March 1943, caring for the sick. During this time she wrote, 'It does not matter how far we are separated from everything, no matter what is taken from us: the faith that we carry in our hearts is something no one can take from us. In this way we build an altar in our own hearts.'[60] She was beheaded on 30 March, which was Tuesday of Holy Week. The final year of her life had been a long Lent of suffering, but she was sustained by her love of the one who hung on the cross, the one she would not deny.

These two martyrs died in their own countries; our next two travelled from Poland to Peru. **Miguel Tomaszek** and **Zbigniew Strzalkowski**, friars and priests, arrived in Peru in the late 1980s. Along with another friar, they served five rural parishes, which had for many years been without any pastoral or sacramental care. The friars in this new mission travelled long distances, often on foot or on horseback, to reach isolated communities. As well as teaching the faith they also initiated social projects in this poor area to provide drinking water and healthcare.

This was a turbulent time in Peru, and a Marxist guerrilla organisation, the Shining Path, was strongly against those who worked for peace. On 9 August 1991 they came after Mass, took Miguel and Zbigniew from their friary, drove them to a place near the cemetery and shot them both. Miguel was 31 and Zbigniew 33. The guerrillas wrote that they killed them because 'they preach peace and tranquillise the people with religion, through the rosary, Masses, reading the Holy Scripture, and because of that, the people don't want revolution. We must kill those who preach peace.'[61]

These two brothers were accidental martyrs, but no less inspiring for that. A Franciscan leader said of them:

> These two Poles were very ordinary Friars, itinerants with sandals planted firmly on the ground. They are our contemporaries. They had their own fears, weaknesses, and anxieties. They did not pray for the grace of martyrdom. It happened. Their faith gave them courage to rise and meet the moment of their destiny – in solidarity with the poor and their fellow

victims of violence. The terrorists burned the bridge, but the Friars' witness doused those flames and galvanised the town to rebuild a bridge of hope.[62]

With our final Franciscans we move into our present century and to the USA. **Mychal Judge** was a friar in New York, where he was born in 1933 to Irish immigrants. After his father's death, when Mychal was six, he shined shoes at Penn Station to make money for his family. There was a Franciscan church across the street, and it was there that his vocation began to develop. In 1954 he became a novice friar and made his life vows in 1958. In 1961 he was ordained as a priest, and in 1986 he returned to the church in Manhattan, where he had first met Franciscans. There was a large friary there, where he lived for the rest of his life.

His ministry was widespread; he was generous with his time and attention, with a particular concern for those whom others ignored or blamed for their difficulty. He had himself had problems with alcohol in the 1970s, becoming sober in 1978 with the help of Alcoholics Anonymous, and he used this experience to help others struggling with addiction. He also had a particular ministry to people with HIV and AIDS at a time when many in the church wouldn't help them. He worked in the city's first AIDS ward, in St Clare's hospital, took the funerals of those who had died and comforted their families. When a man dying of AIDS asked Mychal, 'Do you think God hates me?', he responded by picking him up, kissing him and silently rocking him in his arms.[63] He continued to be an advocate for gay rights for the rest of his life, and there is controversy over whether he himself was gay.

In 1992 he was appointed a chaplain to the New York City Fire Department. There was a fire station immediately across the road from the friary, and his window overlooked it. One of his fellow friars told how, every time the siren sounded and the firefighters left on a call, Mychal, if he was in his room, would go to the window, raise his hand in a blessing and pray for the firefighters.[64] He often went to offer prayer and support at rescues, visited injured firefighters in hospital and supported their families.

He was at the friary on 11 September 2001 when the attack on the Twin Towers took place. As his beloved firefighters rushed to the scene, Mychal Judge went to be with them. He prayed over some who had already died, then went into the lobby of the North Tower, where an emergency command post had been set up. He continued to offer help and prayers there, including anointing a wounded firefighter, until the South Tower collapsed. Debris rained down inside the lobby, killing many, including Mychal. He was 68 years old. Apparently at the moment of his death he was praying loudly, 'Jesus, please end this right now! God, please end this!' His body was found by police and fire officers and carried outside. 'Iconic' has become an overused word, but the image of these dusty rescue workers carrying him out has become one of the most powerful images from that terrible day.[65] Although not the first to be killed, he became the first officially recorded fatality, Victim 0001.

A number of memorials have been created to this friar, including a bronze bust at the fire station which he served. But perhaps his best memorial is a prayer he wrote, which he prayed every day: 'Lord, take me where you want me to go; let me meet who you want me to meet; tell me what you want me to say; and keep me out of your way.'[66] In its down-to-earth realism, the prayer seems to capture his spirit; he lived it out to the end of his life. He may not be a martyr in the traditional sense, but it was his love of God and commitment to serve all God's people that led directly to his death, and for me that means he can be counted among those who laid down their lives for their faith.

Our final Franciscan falls into the same category and is one of my own brothers. **Justus Richard** belonged to the Province of the Americas. Born in Virginia, after finishing college he enlisted in the army and trained as a linguist. However, when he was then sent to Vietnam, he worked as a clerk typist (in a letter he describes this as 'typical army fashion'). He had already visited the SSF brothers and kept in touch with them while in Vietnam. His language skills were not entirely wasted: he writes of taking children from a local orphanage to the zoo in Saigon. And alongside his military service, he was also active in faith, studying to be a lay reader.

When the ceasefire was signed in early 1973 he was discharged and immediately joined SSF to test his vocation, making his life vows in 1979. He went on, like Francis, to be ordained deacon. Eventually he was elected as minister provincial, serving from 1993 to 2002. He was living near New York on 9/11 and volunteered as a chaplain with the Red Cross at Ground Zero, praying over the human remains being recovered and supporting those doing this difficult and stressful work.

When his term of office finished, he asked to go to another province for a time and became the principal of Newton Theological College in Papua New Guinea. He was happy there, writing early in 2005 that he hoped to stay for a further two years. During the Christmas break of 2006 one of the students invited him to return to his own village with him, to meet his family. Justus accepted and set off for the remote village on Mount Hagen. While there, a cold from which he'd been suffering developed into pneumonia and he became gravely ill. There was no hospital nearby and no roads. Men from the village carried him on a stretcher for four hours to reach a medical centre, but he died on the way. It was 13 December, and he was 58 years old. Again Justus may not be a martyr in the traditional sense, but his commitment to God and to his people led him to share the vulnerability of the people he served. An illness which would have been easily treated in a more prosperous country became fatal – as is the case for so many people who die needlessly.

Martyrdom can be long expected or almost accidental, but those who die for their faith, or because of where their faith leads them, are a reminder that both life and death are in God's hands. If we call ourselves Christian, we are putting our whole life, from beginning to end, into God's care.

For reflection

- When you read the stories of those who might have avoided martyrdom – for example, the first Franciscan martyrs, who went against local advice and continued to preach, or Maria Restituta persisting in hanging crucifixes in the hospital – what do you think? Were they brave or foolish? Reflect on these words from Paul: 'For the foolishness of God is wiser than human wisdom, and the weakness of God is stronger than human strength' (1 Corinthians 1:25).

- We've seen how martyrdom and politics are often closely linked, in Ireland, Japan, China and Peru, among many other places. Death can be the cost of becoming involved with the messy realities of life. Are you willing to become caught up in this side of life, perhaps at risk to your reputation or peace of mind, though probably not to your life itself?

- What or who is important enough for you that you would die for it? For many people this would be members of their family, perhaps especially their children. But is there something or someone beyond those blood ties for which you would be willing to give up your life? This might make a good meditation for the season of Lent, when we remember Jesus' willingness to give up his life for us.

7

SHARING THEIR SUPREME TREASURE: MISSIONARIES AND PREACHERS

'Preach the gospel by all means. If necessary use words' has become a very popular quotation from Francis. Sadly there is no evidence that he actually said it. It isn't recorded anywhere in his own writings or in the biographies written soon after his death. However, he might well have agreed with the sentiment, and certainly over the centuries many Franciscans have gone out into the world to share the gospel and to preach the word.

Most of these, as with theologians, have been men; women, as we saw in chapter 3, were excluded from formal theological education, and permission to preach was increasingly confined to priests, who were of course all men. But this did not prevent our first preacher from preaching in the streets of her home town, Viterbo in Italy.

Rose of Viterbo was born around 1233, not long after the death of Francis and while Clare was still alive. When she was three, Franciscan friars arrived in Viterbo, and Rose was captivated by them. She dressed up in a habit tied with a thick rope and insisted on having her hair shaved into the tonsure. She was not just play-acting; from an early age she had a rich spiritual life, seeing visions of townspeople who had died long before she was born, praying regularly and living an ascetic life. Soon she took to the streets and began preaching as the friars did, and people flocked to hear her. She began to bring them home so she could continue to teach. Her parents were unsurprisingly not happy and tried to stop her, but she embraced every difficulty as a chance to imitate Christ, and they allowed her to continue. It isn't recorded what the friars made of her, but they may well have been concerned about the impact of this unconventional young girl on their own ministry.

Rose joined the Third Order in her early teens and a few years later sought to become a Poor Clare in the local monastery, but the nuns refused. She was too controversial a person to fit easily into their community, and in addition her family was too poor to provide the dowry. Had she entered, it would have brought an end to her street ministry; as it was, she continued to live a life of penance and prayer in her family home and of preaching and prophecy outside it. She died on 6 March 1251, aged only 18. A few years later, her body was exhumed and found to be incorrupt and sweet smelling. The people brought her to the Poor Clares, and the community which had refused her entry in life now eagerly received her body.

The Pope himself began a movement to declare Rose a saint, but it seems that some thought her example too risky to promote. In 1253 Clare died, and her less controversial example eclipsed Rose. Clare was soon canonised, while Rose, though seen as a saint in Viterbo, was not declared one by the wider church until 1457. By this time she was no longer remembered for her preaching and prophecy but only for her ascetic acts and deep faith. The unconventional aspects of her life were written out of the official record. Even two centuries later, when a new biography labelled her an 'apostolic preacher', it was placed on the Index of Prohibited Books until the phrase was edited out.

The people of Viterbo, however, continued to remember and value her. When the church was considering declaring her a saint, the locals recounted their stories of her, handed down the generations in oral tradition for two centuries. Her body still lies in the Poor Clare monastery, and it is carried through the town on 4 September, her feast day, and has also been brought out at times of threat, such as earthquake or military attack. The young girl whose deeds and words made such an impact in her short life continues to preach after her death. And in light of her own early death, these words of hers are especially poignant: 'Live so as not to fear death. For those who live well in the world, death is not frightening, but sweet and precious.'[67]

While Rose preached only in her home country, **Odoric of Pordenone** travelled across much of the known world. Unlike the martyrs we met in the previous chapter, he also came safely home again. Odoric was born in northern Italy in the second half of the 13th century; sources vary widely about the date of his birth – 1286 seems most likely, but it could have been a decade or more earlier. He became a Franciscan friar, and around 1317 sailed from Venice as a missionary to Asia, not returning until 1330. Franciscans had been entrusted by successive popes with missions to the east since 1254, perhaps because of Francis' preference for dialogue over crusade, so Odoric was not setting out into entirely unknown territory. But it was a time of turmoil and violence, which saw the rise of the Mongol empire under Genghis Khan. At his death in 1227, only a year after Francis, Genghis Khan's empire 'stretched from Korea to the Persian Gulf, to Georgia, and in the south to India'.[68]

From Constantinople, Odoric moved on to Armenia, Media and Persia (now Iran), where there were already Franciscan mission centres. Travelling to the Persian Gulf he sailed to India, landing in Thane near Mumbai in 1322. Several fellow Franciscan missionaries, led by Thomas of Tolentino, had recently been martyred here. In April 1321, they had been staying with a family, and when a quarrel broke out and the husband beat his wife, they were called as witnesses in the ensuing court case. The judge began a discussion of religion, which led to their condemnation for blaspheming Muhammad.

The martyrs' bodies were buried at Supera, north of Mumbai; Odoric disinterred these relics and carried them with him as he travelled.

Most he finally buried in China, though he brought Thomas of Tolentino's head back to his hometown and to the Franciscans there. That must have been a salutary reminder of the dangers of missionary journeys and of preaching the gospel.

As well as preaching, Odoric also wrote extensively, and was interested in everything he saw as he travelled. In Puri, for example, he witnessed the Chariot Festival of the Hindu god Jagannath and was one of the first to write about it for a western audience. When he left India he sailed to Sumatra, and on to Java and Borneo before arriving in China, where he spent three years, from 1324 to 1327. He travelled widely through the country, ending up in present-day Beijing, then the headquarters of the Great Khan, the emperor of China. There he would undoubtedly have met and served with the Franciscan archbishop, John of Monte Corvino, founder of the earliest Catholic missions in both India and China, and now in his late 70s. The emperor was well disposed towards the Franciscans, and Odoric and Archbishop John took part in a ceremony of blessing the Khan.[69]

Odoric's interest in the life of the people among whom he was living is shown by the fact that he records the practices of cormorant fishing, foot-binding among women and allowing fingernails to grow to extravagant lengths. Other travellers to the east, among them Marco Polo 30 years earlier, though they must have seen these common customs, didn't record them in their writings. This curiosity would undoubtedly have made Odoric a better preacher and evangelist, able to tailor his message to the lives of those to whom he was preaching. He was remarkably open to other cultures and faiths, recording how impressed he was by the size of Chinese cities and their fleets and visiting Buddhist monasteries and Hindu temples. He also loved the food!

Odoric's return to Italy took him overland, perhaps through Mongolia, and in Tibet he may even have visited Lhasa. When he arrived back in Italy, along with Brother James of Ireland, who had accompanied him for at least some of his odyssey, after a journey of more than 50,000 kilometres, he went to the friary in Padua, where he dictated the whole story of his travels to another brother, William of Solagna. Odoric and James then set out to the Pope, then based in Avignon, to report on their missionary journey. Odoric, however, fell ill on the way and returned to Udine, the capital of his native province, where he died in January 1331. His Franciscan brothers were about to bury him simply, but the chief magistrate of the city insisted on a public funeral. Tales of his travels and of posthumous miracles spread rapidly, and the funeral had to be postponed several times, before finally taking place in the presence of the patriarch of Aquileia and all the important local people. The city built a shrine for his body, which became a place of pilgrimage.

Another Franciscan who both travelled and wrote was **Ramon Llull**, whose particular commitment was to mission in the Islamic world. Unlike Odoric of Pordenone, Ramon, who was born on Majorca in 1232, grew up in a multicultural environment. He 'was the son of wealthy Catalan colonists who settled in Majorca after taking part in the conquest of the island by James I of Aragon'.[70] Only a few years before his birth, the Balearic Islands had been retaken by Christian rulers from their Arab rulers. Around a third of the population of Majorca was still Muslim, and it was a major trading centre, with Jewish merchants from North Africa living alongside French and Italian Christians.

Ramon married in 1257 and was a court troubadour and head of the royal household. In his early 30s he experienced a profound conversion and joined the Third Order. From then until his death in his 80s he dedicated his life to an attempt to bring Christians, Muslims and Jews together in God's truth.

He studied Arabic and other languages and travelled widely to persuade those in authority of the importance to missionary work of being able to read and speak the native languages of those they sought to convert. The Franciscans were persuaded first, founding a language school for missionaries at Miramar in Majorca in 1276. Finally, the Council of Vienne in 1311 agreed that Christians undertaking missionary work among Jews and Muslims should learn Hebrew and Arabic, and ordered the creation of chairs in these languages in a number of European universities.

But Ramon did not only seek to prepare others for missionary work; he also undertook it himself. He produced Christian books for Muslims to read and travelled widely through Europe, Palestine and North Africa, preaching the love of Christ. As well as preaching his own sermons, he wrote textbooks on the preparation of sermons.

After spending time in Tunis, he believed that the conversion of Muslims should be achieved through prayer and not through war and violence. He wrote:

> I see many knights going to the Holy Land beyond the seas… thinking… they can acquire it by force of arms; but in the end all are destroyed… It seems to me that the conquest of the Holy Land ought not to be attempted except in the way in which You and your apostles acquired it, namely, by love and prayers, and the pouring out of tears and of blood.[71]

Violence, however, marked the end of his own life. At the age of 82 he travelled again to Tunis to preach the Christian faith and was imprisoned there. On his release in 1315 he was stoned by an angry crowd but rescued by Christians in the city and taken back to Majorca by Genoese merchants, where he died in 1316, aged 84. He is an important inspiration for those involved in dialogue between the three Abrahamic faiths and also a reminder of the importance for all missionaries, at home or abroad, of understanding and being able to speak the language of those they want to reach, whether that is literally another language or more subtly having an understanding of the words and ideas that will speak to their concerns.

Missionary work and preaching were major enterprises of the Franciscan friars for many centuries, initially in Europe and then, following European exploration across the Atlantic, in the Americas. While many wanted to go abroad, far more often their preaching was to those in Europe who were already at least nominally Christian. They sought to strengthen their faith and to rekindle the faith of those who had become lukewarm. Two of the most famous of these were Anthony of Padua and Bernardine of Siena.

We met **Anthony of Padua** briefly in the previous chapter. As a young Augustinian monk in Portugal he was moved to become a Franciscan by the return of the bodies of the first Franciscan martyrs to the friary in Coimbra in 1220. His great knowledge of scripture informed his powerful preaching, mainly in northern Italy and southern France, and he was given permission by Francis himself to teach the friars. His Franciscan heart can be seen in the way that he emphasised the link between conversion to the gospel and social justice. He did this not only in his sermons, but also in practical ways. For example, he persuaded the government in Padua to change the way in which people in debt were treated. Instead of being imprisoned, which meant their situation could not change, they could now declare themselves bankrupt, which allowed them to start a new life.

Anthony preached before the Pope and cardinals in a church council, where it's recorded that in an echo of the day of Pentecost (Acts 2) all those present, from many countries, heard him in their own languages, and 'the Pope, amazed at the profound things set before them from the Holy Scriptures by Saint Antony, said, "He is truly 'the Ark of the Covenant' and 'the repository of Holy Scripture.'"'[72] Anthony died in Padua in 1231, aged 36.

Another of the great Franciscan preachers, **Bernardine of Siena**, was born in 1380 in Tuscany to a noble family. He was orphaned young, but under the care of several aunts received an excellent education. In 1400, Siena suffered a severe plague, and Bernardine along with a few companions volunteered to run the city's largest hospital.

This experience led him to decide to devote his life to God, and he joined a new Franciscan group, the Observant reform, in 1403. Like Anthony, he studied the scriptures in depth, and he travelled widely in northern and central Italy, preaching in an energetic and accessible way. Also like Anthony, he addressed issues of social justice in his sermons.

Bernardine's greatest legacy to the church was his devotion to the holy name of Jesus; when he preached he held up a plaque with the initials 'I.H.S.', an acronym for the name of Jesus. In one of his sermons, he said:

> The name of Jesus is the glory of preachers, because the shining splendour of that name causes his word to be proclaimed and heard. And how do you think such an immense, sudden and dazzling light of faith came into the world, if not because Jesus was preached? Was it not through the brilliance and sweet savour of this name that God *called us into his marvelous light*?[73]

As well as his gifts as a preacher, Bernardine also led the friars of the Observant reform for some years. During his time as a friar the group grew from about 130 to over 4,000 members in Italy. He continued to travel and to preach until his death in 1444.

More than two centuries later, another Italian dedicated his life to preaching in his own country. **Leonard of Port Maurice** was born in 1676 and became a friar in 1697. After his ordination, he wanted to become a missionary in China, but his health was poor and his superiors refused to send him abroad. For the remaining 40 years of his life he sought, through parish missions, Lenten sermons and retreats, to convert his hearers to a deeper and more authentic Christian life. Like Bernardine, he preached devotion to the holy name of Jesus, but his particular devotion was to the way of the cross, and he erected over 500 sets of stations of the cross throughout Italy. The most famous of these was in the Colosseum in Rome, where early Christians had been martyred. About this devotion he wrote:

What salutary insights will the continued meditation on the bitter passion of the Son of God stir up in the soul! Daily experience has taught me that by this devout form of prayer people's lives are quickly changed for the better. For the Way of the Cross is the antidote for vice, the cleansing of unbridled desires and an effective incentive to virtue and holiness of life.[74]

Despite his poor health, Leonard lived to the age of 75, dying in the friary in Rome where he had become a Franciscan.

Others were able to fulfil their desire for mission work abroad. One of these was **Francis Solano**, an aristocratic Spaniard who joined the Franciscans in 1569 aged 20. In 1576 he was ordained, and he became a wandering preacher in Andalusian villages. When an epidemic broke out, he nursed the sick with no thought for his own health. In 1589, he volunteered to be a missionary to South America and was sent to bring the gospel to the indigenous peoples of what is now north-west Argentina, the Gran Chaco region of Bolivia, and Paraguay. He was a successful missionary, learning a number of native languages and, as a violinist, also using music in his work. Many stories were told of the miracles he worked.

In 1601 he moved to Lima, to be guardian of the friary there, and he worked not to convert but to recall nominal Christians to a more committed practice of their faith. He died in Lima in 1610, but today, more than four centuries later, there is still great devotion to him in Argentina, Bolivia, Chile, Paraguay and Peru. In the Argentinian town of Humuhuaca, a mechanical statue of the saint emerges from the church every day at noon to bless the people.[75]

In time the dedicated work of missionaries bore fruit, and local Christians took up the work of evangelism and preaching. One of these was **Frei Galvao**, the first Brazilian to be declared a saint. He was educated by the Jesuits but chose to join the Franciscans in 1755, at the age of 16, and spent most of his life in the city of São Paulo, with a ministry focused on preaching, prayer and outreach to the poor and needy. He had a reputation as a healer, and many people asked for his prayer. He died in 1822 and was canonised in 2007. He is an example of the positive effects of missionary work in growing the indigenous church.

However, this work has also been controversial, as seen especially in the life of **Junipero Serra**. Like Ramon Llull, he was born on Majorca, in 1713, and became a friar there. He was academically brilliant, and after his own ordination in 1737 he taught the philosophy and theology of Duns Scotus (see chapter 3) to student friars. In 1749 he abandoned this comfortable life and volunteered for mission work among the indigenous peoples of America. Arriving in Mexico, he refused the horse supplied by royal officials and walked to Mexico City, where he joined the Missionary College of San Fernando. Within a year he was sent out to run a mission among the Pame people. He sought to strengthen their Christian life as recent converts, but also to support their farming, spinning and other practical work so that they could support themselves. In 1758 he returned to the college, where he worked in administration as well as undertaking missionary journeys over a wide area.

In 1767, aged 54, he began the work which would make his name and also make him controversial. The king of Spain expelled the Jesuits from Baja (Southern) California, where they had been working for 70 years, and the Franciscans stepped in. Junipero was put in charge of this new mission, which later extended into Alta (Northern) California. He eventually founded nine missions, from San Diego in the south to San Francisco in the north, and died at the mission at Carmel in 1784. He was canonised in 2015, but not without protest by some native American groups, who believed that the missionaries had virtually enslaved those they converted.

The situation was complicated by the overlap between Spanish colonial expansion and Franciscan missionary zeal. An article written by Thomas Reese at the time of Serra's canonisation explains:

Under the Spanish system, the missionaries were paid by the government, so missionaries were both church and state functionaries. From the point of view of the church, the purpose of the missions was to spread the Gospel to those who had not been baptised. From the point of view of the state, the missions were institutions aimed at assimilating the native peoples, making them citizens of the empire. That meant, among other things, learning European-style agriculture, becoming a Catholic, and living in a congregated pueblo-type arrangement, just like people in Spain. A great deal of the tension in the mission system stemmed from this double purpose, for these two aims did not always coexist easily with each other.[76]

The Franciscan missionaries thought that they had a duty to protect the native people from exploitation from ranchers, miners, settlers and soldiers, which was a real risk. But in order to do this they did not allow those they baptised to leave the mission; if they left without permission they were pursued and brought back. It was a paternal-istic attitude, which was probably held by 99% of settlers of the time, who saw the native Americans as akin to children, though certainly as people and not as property. After Serra's death the colonial and mission systems became more and more interdependent, with the settlers relying on food supplied by the missions, who had to find more and more 'converts' to keep up production. Herding large groups of people together led to the spread of disease and a high death rate.

But it is unfair to blame the whole later history of the missions on Junipero Serra, who had a genuine passion to reach those who had not heard the gospel. The reality was that the colonial powers would have come anyway, and the missionaries believed that by being involved they could mitigate some of the harsher effects of colonisation. Later history includes grim examples of colonial expansion without missionary involvement:

The example of Indian removal from many regions in the 19th century U.S. is a grim instance. In fact, if there was genocide against native peoples in California, it happened during the gold rush, in the 1850s, when Americans offered bounties for Indian scalps and the native peoples of Northern California were brutally decimated and oppressed.[77]

The example of Junipero Serra is a reminder that missionary work is complex and often a matter of weighing up difficult choices. It cannot be separated from the political and economic realities of life.

The rules of the Catholic church continued to make it impossible for women to be preachers, but as the religious life changed and developed, and women were able to exercise an active ministry, they did serve as missionaries. One of the largest of these congregations in the Catholic church today is the Franciscan Missionaries of Mary (FMM), whom we met in chapter 6, and it's with two of their sisters that this chapter continues.

The community was founded in 1877 in British India, by a French woman, **Mary of the Passion**. She was drawn to the Franciscan way of life and briefly entered a Poor Clare monastery in her home town of Nantes. Ill health meant she had to leave, and when she recovered she joined another community, who sent her to India to help to establish a native congregation of sisters. In India she made her life vows, aged 28, and became provincial superior. However, in 1876 troubles in the community reached such a pitch that it split; 20 of the 33 sisters left with Mary of the Passion and formed a new community, dedicated solely to missionary work. This included medical care for local people, especially women, who could not access medical care provided by men. A novitiate was opened in France, and many women joined in order to serve overseas.

It was not until 1882 that Mary returned to her Franciscan roots. On a visit to Rome she met the minister general of the Order of Friars Minor and joined the Third Order. Three years later the new community adopted a Franciscan rule and became the Franciscan Missionaries of Mary. Sisters were sent out to a number of countries, including China, where in 1900, as we saw in the previous chapter, all seven sisters were martyred. Four years later, Mary of the Passion, still superior general, died at the age of 65. She left behind 2,000 Franciscan Missionaries of Mary on four continents.

Less than a year later, another sister of her community died, aged only 26. **Maria Assunta Pallotta**, born in 1878 in Italy, was the eldest of five children and the only girl. By the time she was 11 her father had left the family home to find work, and Maria Assunta had to take on new responsibilities to help her mother. She had already left school, having received only two years of education. When she was 20, she left home to join the FMM, undertaking manual work such as cooking, caring for animals and harvesting olives. At the beginning of 1904 she made a request to go to China to work in the missions; in February she made her life vows and not long after was told she would indeed be going to China, to the house where the martyrs had lived. After a three-month journey she arrived, working as an orphanage cook and learning to speak Mandarin.

Within a year of her arrival an epidemic of typhus broke out; she was tireless in nursing the sick, until she herself was diagnosed with the disease. She died on 7 April 1905. The room in which she lay was filled with a wonderful fragrance, which remained for three days until her funeral and burial. In January 1904 Maria Assunta wrote to her parents that she asked God for 'the grace to make known to the world purity of intention which consists in doing all for the Love of God, even the most ordinary actions'.[78] Her short and outwardly unheroic life shows that God answered her prayer. Missionary work may be very public and visible, or it may be hidden, carried out quietly in an orphanage kitchen or a sickroom. It is the motivation that makes it a work of mission.

In my own community mission has been domestic far more often than it has involved travelling abroad. Brothers from the UK did make the long voyage to Papua New Guinea in 1959, and later to the Solomon Islands, with the aim of founding Franciscan communities there rather than carrying out primary evangelism. And a number of brothers have supported indigenous African communities over the years, living with them and seeking to encourage local leadership.

For many years parish mission was a major element in our ministry, with teams of brothers and sisters, often joined by tertiaries, spending up to a fortnight in parishes, teaching and preaching, talking over meals and seeking to strengthen the faith of the faithful and to draw in those on the margins of faith. Changes in parish life and a reduction in our own numbers have made this less central today. However, individuals are still asked to preach, to lead quiet days or retreats or simply to visit parishes.

Francis wrote in his Earlier Rule that there were two ways in which his brothers could witness to their faith:

> One way is not to engage in arguments or disputes but to be subject to every human creature for God's sake and to acknowledge that they are Christians. The other way is to announce the Word of God, when they see it pleases the Lord.[79]

Our Principles echo this, saying, 'The witness of life is more eloquent than that of words.' In a number of places sisters and brothers are following this first way, living in multifaith areas in Leicester, Leeds and London, being good neighbours and being known as Christians. This, as much as preaching the word of God, is mission. Those around us do notice how we live, perhaps more than we realise. I remember, when I lived in Brixton in the early 1990s, a neighbour saying how much they valued seeing the light coming on in the room we used as a chapel and knowing that we were praying. Living our lives faithfully is a witness to what we believe and to what we value, at least as much as preaching, which may often be heard only by the already believing. Francis offers a no less demanding but equally authentic way of engaging in mission.

For reflection

- Rose of Viterbo had a strong sense of calling from a very young age. How seriously do we take the faith of children? Can you find ways in your church community and family home of including them and their gifts more fully?

- How curious are you about other cultures and faiths? Are you stimulated by difference or threatened by it? How might you take on more of the spirit of Odoric of Pordenone?

- Ramon Llull was determined that missionaries should learn to speak the language of the people to whom they were sent. How committed are you, and we as a church, to learning to speak in 'languages' that enable us to be heard? This may be literal languages or, more metaphorically, being able to communicate to those we seek to reach with the gospel in ways they can understand and respond to.

- Bernardine of Siena and the holy name of Jesus; Leonard of Port Maurice and the stations of the cross – what devotion or religious practice would you especially recommend to others?

- The work of Junipero Serra towards the end of his life raises some difficult questions about missionary work. Reread that section and reflect on it. What might be today's quandaries? For example, is it right to work to convert people in countries where the dominant faith does not accept conversion to another faith as legitimate?

- Do you see the ordinary things you do for the love of God as 'missionary'? If not, what prevents you? And how might you move in this direction? Perhaps you might choose to start each day consciously dedicating all your activities to God and see what difference this makes.

- If you could preach just one sermon, what would you say? What is the core of the gospel for you?

8

LOVING WITH HIS LOVE: PASTORS

While preachers and missionaries are public, and their ministry obvious to all, the Franciscans included in this chapter had a much more individual and private calling. They are the ones who guided others on their spiritual journey, comforted the grieving and accompanied the lonely. This ministry has often been part of priesthood, and many of those whose names we know were ordained, which means they are mainly men. However, this ministry of listening, sharing wisdom, disentangling perplexity, comforting the afflicted and afflicting the comfortable has also been widely exercised by Franciscan women, including those living the enclosed life. The convent parlour has often been a place of such encounter.

Our first pastor is one of Francis' early companions, **Giles**. He was a farm labourer who was the third man to join Francis, in 1208, aged 18. He spent much of his early life as a brother travelling and going on pilgrimage, witnessing to his own conversion by his example of prayer and hard work, along with simple words. In 1219 he travelled to Tunis in North Africa, just a short time before the first Franciscans were martyred in Morocco. Giles was always happy to turn his hand to whatever work was needed, from cutting wood and carrying water to burying the dead. And he was a keen observer of those around him, observation which he turned to brief words of wisdom. As he grew older, Giles devoted himself to prayer and moved to a hermitage near Perugia, where he stayed until his death in 1262, aged over 70. When Bonaventure (see chapter 3) was writing his biography of Francis, the *Major Legend*, he visited Giles to gather stories of the early days.

As we saw in chapter 5, King Louis of France visited Giles on one of his pilgrimages, but many others, from all walks of life, also came to visit Giles and seek his wisdom. Those around him collected his sayings, which are very down to earth, with an emphasis on the necessity of putting faith into action. Here are two examples:

> Sometimes we try to learn many things so as to be useful to others, but study few things helpful to ourselves.

> He once said to a certain person who wished to get some schooling and become learned: 'Why do you want to attend school? The sum of all knowledge is this: to fear and love God. These two things should satisfy you. A person has as much wisdom as he puts to good use and no more. So don't put great emphasis on your learning. Try, with full enthusiasm to do something productive, and then you can be confident in what you have accomplished.'[80]

Giles had a reputation for not mincing his words in his sermons, and if his recorded sayings can be trusted his individual advice was the same. The ministry of a pastor is to challenge as well as to comfort and encourage.

Another solitary friar with a ministry to others was **John Joseph of the Cross**. Born in southern Italy in 1654 to an aristocratic family, he gave it all up at the age of 16 to join a very austere group of Franciscans, becoming their leader in 1702. He always went barefoot and wore the same habit for his entire life; it had so many patches that he became known as 'the friar of a hundred pieces'. His austere life, however, did not make him unhappy; on the contrary, he was known for his cheerfulness. Neither did it make him harsh to others, for he also had a reputation for being a compassionate confessor, with great gifts of discernment. At the monastery he founded he also built a small, more contemplative house, an hour's walk away, which he called St Mary of the Needy. Brothers could spend time there in deep prayer and solitude, but always this was to be balanced with a return to active ministry. John Joseph wrote that Francis wanted his followers to withdraw to hermitages, 'so that, by living alone with God and by themselves for a time, they could then leave them prepared to bring good to others without harming their own souls'.[81]

When John Joseph was declared a saint in 1839, a century after his death, two of those canonised with him were Alphonsus Ligouri, bishop and founder of another religious community, the Redemptorists, and the Jesuit Francis of Geronimo, who had both chosen him as their spiritual director. His embrace of poverty and of solitude had not removed him from a powerful and fruitful pastoral ministry to others.

We next turn to two women whose lives as enclosed sisters likewise did not prevent them from being highly valued advisors and counsellors. **Maria Crescentia Hoss** was a Bavarian weaver who longed to join the enclosed Third Order Franciscan sisters in her home town of Kaufbeuren. But her father, also a weaver, was too poor to give the necessary dowry. When Maria was 21 the mayor, a Protestant, bought a tavern next to the convent, which had been a source of disturbance, and gave it to the nuns. He asked that in return Maria be admitted. The superior, resenting this, treated her badly, using her as a servant and even leaving her without a cell of her own. A new superior four years later was more sympathetic and made her first portress and then mistress of novices. As well as forming new members of the community, she also wrote many letters to people of all sorts, giving them advice and comfort. Visitors also came to see her in person:

> Both simple men and women, princes and empresses, priests and religious, abbots and bishops. In a certain way she became a kind of "midwife" and helped those seeking counsel to bring forth the truth in their hearts.[82]

For the last three years of Maria's life, before her death on Easter Sunday 1744, aged 61, she was herself the superior, and she sought to renew the life of her community, encouraging her sisters to turn to the gospels to enrich and grow their spiritual life, to love silence and mutual service and to trust unreservedly in God's providence.

Mary Magdalene Martinengo was a contemporary of Maria Cresentia Hoss, being born five years after her in northern Italy. Her family was well-to-do, but her childhood was difficult. Her mother died when Mary was only five months old, and she herself suffered poor health until the age of five. From the age of 11 she attended convent boarding schools, which was normal for a girl from her background. She began to feel an attraction towards the enclosed contemplative life, but her father had promised her in marriage to the son of a Venetian senator. Her brothers gave her romantic novels to read and beautiful dresses, and she was torn between her love of these things and her desire for God. By the time she was 18 she was determined to join the Capuchin Poor Clares and finally overcame her father's resistance. However, he arranged a tour of Italian cities for her before she entered, a common custom at the time, giving her a final chance to change her mind. She entered the Monastery of Saint Mary of the Snows (Santa Maria delle Neve) in September 1705 and made life vows a year later.

For the remaining 31 years her external life was mainly very mundane, made up of manual work, including being dishwasher, baker, sweeper, laundress, shoemaker and seamstress. Like Maria, she also held the roles of portress, novice mistress and finally abbess. But her inner life was anything but mundane, combining deep contemplative prayer and mystical experiences with severe spiritual trials and terrible physical suffering. She kept this life hidden from almost everyone; even her confessors and spiritual directors were not entirely aware of it.

Although she was harsh to herself, she was very gentle to others, and her fame brought many people to the monastery to speak to her. She seems to have had the gift of reading deep into the souls of those who came seeking her advice and help, and even of foretelling future events. She used her own experience and her God-given gifts to encourage the disheartened, to call sinners back to the path of faith and to reconcile those at odds with one another. Worn out by her austere and hard-working life, Mary Magdalene died in 1737, aged 50. Even as she lay dying, she was thinking of others. A basket of berries was in front of her, and she took fruit from it and placed the berries in the mouths of her sisters, weeping around her bedside.

On her first visit to the Capuchin sisters, Mary Magdalene had said simply, 'I want to become holy.' In one of her many writings, a treatise on humility, she expanded on this:

> God himself wants us to acquire a high degree of holiness. He made his desire known in saying, 'You shall be holy because I am holy'; and before his passion Jesus raised his eyes and hands to his Father and prayed, 'Holy Father, sanctify them in truth.' Rise up, then, my soul, and be immersed in this sea of holiness and never leave it so that you may be made holy by God's own holiness.[83]

In different times these two women might have been ordained as priests, but whether priests or not, a pattern is beginning to emerge: a life of limitation, whether chosen solitude or enclosed community life, seems often to be a good foundation for pastoral service.

Our next pastor was a priest, and in fact is the patron of parish priests in the Catholic church. But **Jean-Baptiste-Marie Vianney** also struggled with difficult and limiting circumstances, beginning with his birth into a poor farming family in France just before the French Revolution. His family had to maintain their faith in the face of the anti-religious policies of the revolutionary government. Jean spent much of his childhood working as a shepherd, and his lack of formal education made it difficult for him to complete the studies necessary to become a priest. It was not until he was 30, in 1816, that he was finally ordained. After three years he was sent to the village of Ars, near Lyons, a small settlement of about 300 inhabitants, and remained there for the rest of his life. At some point he joined the Third Order.

Initially Jean struggled: his people were apathetic and uninterested in faith. But his own example of authentic Christian life and his commitment to them, especially to the poor and needy, won them over. As the years passed his reputation, especially as a confessor, spread more widely. Like Mary Magdalene Martinengo, he had the ability to discern what was not being said by those who came seeking his counsel, as well as the wisdom to address the problems and pains they presented to him. He also had a sense of humour and became famous for his preaching as well as for his pastoral ministry.

For many years Jean, or the Cure d'Ars, as he became known, preached at 11.00 am, then spent long hours in the confessional, up to 16 hours a day at times. By the 1850s between 15,000 and 20,000 people a year were flocking to the village to seek the counsel of this poor priest, whose compassion for the struggles of his penitents often brought him to tears. His prayers of intercession brought miraculous results.

Jean Vianney was sustained in this demanding ministry by a deep commitment to and delight in prayer. He wrote:

> My children, I know your hearts are small, but prayer will enlarge them and make them capable of loving God. Prayer is a foretaste of heaven, an overflowing of heaven. It never leaves us without sweetness; it is like honey, running down into the soul and sweetening everything with which it comes into contact. When we pray truly, difficulties melt like snow in the sunshine.[84]

Jean was offered various promotions in the church and also felt a call to the religious life, but out of love for his people in Ars he refused them all and remained as a parish priest until his death in 1859.

Another Franciscan with a particular ministry in the confessional was **Leopold Mandic** of Herceg Novi (Castelnuovo in Italian). Born Bogdan Mandic in 1866, in what is now Montenegro, into a noble family impoverished by the political struggles of the time, he left home aged 15 to travel to Italy. Capuchin Franciscan friars had a church in his home town and he longed to join them. A year later he was received into the order and given the name Leopold. He was not on the face of it a likely candidate to be a friar: he was only 4'5" tall, walked with a limp and spoke with a stammer. His hope was to return to his homeland as a missionary, working for the reconciliation of the Catholic and Orthodox churches, but he was prevented from doing so by his physical limitations.

Instead, through persevering in the face of his difficulties, he developed great spiritual strength and depth and spent most of his life hearing confessions, especially in Padua, where he was based for almost 40 years. It might have been easy for this to have become rather routine, but Leopold 'transformed the confessional into an experience of human dignity, a personal encounter of compassion, respect and understanding'.[85] He believed utterly in the mercy of God, and said, 'Some say that I am too good. But if you come and kneel before me, is not this sufficient proof that you want to have God's pardon? God's mercy is beyond all expectation.'[86]

He shared in this merciful nature of God. He would often say to penitents, 'Be at peace; place everything on my shoulders. I will take care of it.' And he explained, 'I give my penitents only small penances because I do the rest myself.'[87] As he became older Leopold developed crippling arthritis, but continued to spend up to 12 hours a day hearing confessions. He died of cancer in Padua in 1942.

Our next pastor is probably one of the best known; he also faced difficulties and has generated considerable controversy. **Francesco Forgione** was born to a poor family in southern Italy in 1887. Like Leopold he wanted to become a Capuchin; like the Cure d'Ars his lack of education was a problem. Francesco's father went to the

USA to work, sending back money to pay for his son's schooling. Francesco entered as a novice in 1903 and was given the name Pio, making his life vows in 1907. In 1910 he became a priest, despite being plagued with poor health. Prayer was at the heart of his life, and when he celebrated the Eucharist there were often long periods of contemplative silence.

Initially, because of his poor health he stayed in his home town, but in 1916 he was sent to a small friary in Apulia, in the town of San Giovanni Rotondo, and stayed there for most of his life, apart from sporadic periods of military service during World War I. It was here in 1918 that he received the stigmata, the signs of Christ's crucifixion in his own body, as Francis himself had. This caused suspicion for a number of years; in the early 1920s he was prevented from hearing confessions and saying Mass, and until the early 1930s the Holy See denied in statements that God was the cause of the unusual events in his life. But when the Vatican tried to have him moved to another friary, in northern Italy, the local people threatened to riot, and the Vatican backed down.

This is a powerful demonstration that his deep spirituality and his gifts of discernment and of reading hearts was already drawing many, initially from his parish but then much more widely, to this small town to be present at his Eucharist and to make their confession to him. He slept and ate very little and rarely left the monastery.

Padre Pio, as he became universally known, had other spiritual gifts, including healing, prophecy, the gift of tongues and, more controversially, miracles and bilocation (the ability to be in two places at once). The wounds of the stigmata gave off a fragrance, which people believed they smelt when he was present but not visible. He was very humble about them; when a friend questioned him about them, he simply replied, 'You know, they are a mystery to me too.'

In the 1950s the friars built a new bigger church to accommodate the large crowds who came to see Padre Pio. These included the curious as well as the convinced. Graham Greene, the novelist, attended one of his Masses and afterwards carried two pictures of him in his wallet. He said that the friar 'had introduced a doubt into my disbelief'.[88] In 1947 the future Pope John Paul II, then a young priest in Poland, travelled to San Giovanni Rotondo to make his confession to Padre Pio, and in 1962 he wrote asking for prayers for a gravely ill friend of his, who was cured.

Padre Pio died in September 1968, aged 81. His funeral was attended by over 100,000 people. Three years later Pope Paul VI said:

> Look what fame he had, what a worldwide following gathered around him! But why? Perhaps because he was a philosopher? Because he was wise? Because he had resources at his disposal? Because he said Mass humbly, heard confessions from dawn to dusk and was – it is not easy to say it – one who bore the wounds of our Lord. He was a man of prayer and suffering.[89]

Padre Pio was canonised in 2002 by Pope John Paul II, and his shrine draws around 8 million pilgrims a year. He remains an inspiration to many and a controversial figure to some. But his advice to penitents, resting on great confidence in the love of God, 'Pray. Hope. Don't worry', is surely a gift many of us need to take to heart.

In 2017, another Capuchin friar, **Solanus Casey**, was beatified, one step on the way to being declared a saint. He was born in 1870, the sixth of 16 children to Irish immigrants in Wisconsin, USA. As with so many of these pastors, he struggled academically; he began studies for the priesthood aged 21 but was advised to join a religious order instead. In 1897 he joined the Capuchins in Detroit and was finally ordained in 1904, but he was only allowed to celebrate Mass and not to hear confessions or preach sermons. He served in New York for 20 years, but in 1924 was transferred back to Detroit, where he began his ministry as porter (doorkeeper) of St Bonaventure Monastery. His job gave him the opportunity to minister with compassion and holiness to the many people who came to the friary seeking help.

He led services for the sick and gave wise advice. In 1929 he helped establish a soup kitchen to feed the hungry during the Depression, a ministry which continues today, and he worked in it for many years. His gift was one of presence and, once again, of many years settled in one place. Gradually people came from far and wide to speak to him and ask for his advice and his prayers.

His teaching was simple, based around gratitude to God; he encouraged those who came not only to thank God for gifts and blessings received, but also to thank him 'ahead of time' for blessings they were yet to receive. His definition of spirituality was, 'The science of our happy relationship and our providential dependence on God and our neighbour.'[90]

Father Solanus died on 31 July 1957. During his final illness he remarked, 'I'm offering my sufferings that all might be one. If only I could see the conversion of the whole world.'[91] He had certainly done his best in his own part of the world to bring about that conversion, in simple but profound ways.

Because of the intimate and confidential nature of pastoral encounters, it's harder to write about this ministry in the lives of my Franciscan sisters and brothers in any great detail. In some measure it's woven into the lives of most of us. The habit, while it can make some people give us a wide berth, draws others to us, to share a present sorrow or perplexity, an ancient hurt or just sometimes a cause for thanksgiving. Simply listening is a gift, one which many people have few opportunities to receive.

There are the one-off encounters in the course of leading quiet days or retreats or taking part in missions. I always offer people the opportunity to come and talk to me about anything the day has brought up. Sometimes this is directly linked to the subject of the day, but it can be absolutely anything. When that door opens and someone appears, I always send up a silent prayer, 'Lord, let me listen with your ears and respond from your heart.' Being rather on the edge of the 'system' can be a strength. People with concerns or difficulties in their parish life feel safe talking to someone unofficial, as also do many clergy, who may not want to share their problem with someone within the diocesan structure.

For some, this pastoral ministry of listening, spiritual direction, hearing confessions and counselling becomes a major part of life. At its simplest it's people coming to talk about their spiritual life, but it has also extended into various forms of chaplaincy, especially in hospitals and prisons. Those may end with retirement, but listening can continue into old age and infirmity. One of my own sisters, **Angela Helen**, had an extensive and much-valued ministry of spiritual direction, which she was able to continue for some years after being diagnosed with multiple sclerosis and becoming a wheelchair user.

Of course, to those who benefit from this ministry, the one offering it seems altogether wonderful. Those who live with the sister or brother may see a different side of them; the image of the 'wounded healer' is an accurate one, and it often seems to be those who bear their own scars who are most skilled at healing those of others.

Ramon, whom we met in chapter 4, had an extensive ministry of spiritual teaching and preaching. After he embraced a solitary life, this ministry continued by letter, but he did not keep the letters and those still in existence at his death were destroyed. However, a flavour of them can be found in some of the letters he wrote to a close friend, Ron Powell, who allowed some to be published in Arthur Howell's book, *A Franciscan Way of Life* (BRF, 2018). While these letters are inevitably only those that he was willing to share, they give a glimpse of Ramon's ongoing pastoral ministry. There is also a glimpse of the one-off encounters he entered into fully, as he travelled by hitchhiking:

A lorry driver giving him a lift would soon pour out his difficulties and problems, for the brown habit was no barrier as the jovial wearer frequently laughed at himself and the newly found friend warmed to him. He had this extraordinary quality of listening intently and discerning precisely what needed to be said, and of encouraging people to share their fears and, above all, to know that God loved them.[92]

This desire to share God's love and mercy is a thread running through the life story of so many of our pastors, one which stretches back to Francis and Clare themselves and the encounters which shaped their own lives and discipleship.

For reflection

- Can you think of a time when you were helped by someone simply listening to you? Give thanks to God for them.

- Have you ever experienced 'knowing' something about another person without being aware of how? How might you use this gift wisely, in the service of God?

- A number of those we met in this chapter spent most of their life in one place, and some also had physical or educational limitations. What do you believe is the particular value of a long ministry in one place? And can limitation produce wisdom on its own, or will formal learning and varied experience always trump it? Do you have experience of this? If you experience limitations in your own life preventing you from carrying out a ministry to which you feel called, take the frustration and sense of loss into prayer and see what happens.

- Have you ever made confession to another Christian, whether formally or informally? How did it affect you? If you were explaining its value to someone else, what would you say?

- We all carry wounds; can you think of a time or times when your own woundedness has enabled you to help someone else? Or might you be using your scars as a reason not to take up a particular ministry? Ask God to show you the way forward.

9

THE WITNESS OF LIFE: SIMPLY LIVING

This final chapter is perhaps the most important of all, but it has also been the most difficult to write. It includes all those who are not well known, who didn't write important books or guide many in prayer; they didn't make heroic missionary journeys, preach life-changing sermons or give their lives as martyrs.

These are the men and women who 'simply lived' a life inspired by Francis and Clare. And they may be the ones who most readily inspire us to do the same. Our Principles say, 'In this task of showing Christ to others, the witness of life is more eloquent than that of words.' Perhaps Mary, to whom both Francis and Clare had a deep devotion, is a model for these people, and in turn to us. Frances Young writes of 'Mary as the model of all those who live ordinary lives, simple and hidden, fulfilling everyday tasks, in communion with Jesus'.[93]

Of course these are only a small sample of the many who have lived like this, and they are unrepresentative in having been remembered at all. Behind them lie many anonymous and forgotten followers, whose witness has been lost, but who are no less important for that.

Agnes of Assisi is the first, and we know a little more about her because she was the sister of Clare. She is inevitably rather in her elder sister's shadow, but she had her own journey of faith. Baptised Catherine, she joined Clare very soon after she had herself left her family to join Francis. The family had given up hope of dissuading

Clare from her path, but they were not willing to let Catherine go as well. A band of men came to the convent where the two women were staying and tried to take her home by force. Clare prayed fervently, and her sister became so heavy that the men could not lift her. Frustrated, they went home, and Francis received Catherine as a sister, giving her the name Agnes. Together Clare and Agnes moved to San Damiano and began the first community of Poor Clares.

Later, in the late 1220s, Agnes was sent to be abbess of another Poor Clare community in Monticello, Florence. She struggled with the separation from Clare and the sisters with whom she had hoped to spend her entire life, and in a letter of around 1230 eloquently expresses her distress and her expectation that she would never see them again. However, after about 20 years she did return to San Damiano and was with Clare on her deathbed. Clare assured her distressed sister that she would soon follow her, and this did in fact happen. Agnes may seem a rather dependent character, but she had the strength to choose to follow Clare despite her family's opposition and to spend 20 years of her life responsible for another community, with few opportunities to communicate with her beloved sister and no opportunities to meet. The two were united in a common vocation, and they lived and died that vocation together.

Another Agnes was also inspired by Clare – **Agnes of Prague**. A princess, sister of King Wenceslaus and first cousin to Elizabeth of Hungary, she was destined to make a politically advantageous marriage. However, two attempts failed, and she turned to her own path. When she was 21 Franciscan friars came to Prague, and she was drawn to their preaching and values. After founding a church and a friary, she endowed a hospital with her dowry. Finally, she invited Poor Clare sisters from Italy to establish a community in Prague, which she entered in 1234, aged 23. This inspired Clare to write to her, and we have four precious letters from the next 20 years, which are key sources for our knowledge of Clare. Sadly, we have no letters from Agnes to Clare, so she remains a shadowy figure. But she was faithful to her initial decision and determined to follow Clare's vision of Franciscan life, and she led her community until her death in 1282.

Born around 1285, **Sancia of Naples** also came from a royal family. She is connected to the kings, queens and princes we met in chapter 5, and perhaps it's hard to see her as having lived a 'simple life'. But on her own terms she lived a fairly ordinary life, and has never been recognised by the church as especially holy. As we have already seen, the royal families of Europe were very much interconnected, and Sancia had Elizabeth of Hungary as her great-aunt, Louis of Toulouse as her brother-in-law and James of Majorca as her brother.

Not surprisingly, given these connections, it seemed that Sancia always had a longing to dedicate her life to God, and she sought permission to become a nun from an early age. Being a member of the royal family of Majorca, this was denied her, and instead in 1304 she was married to Robert, of the House of Anjou, brother of Louis of Toulouse. Because Louis renounced his own royal inheritance, Robert became king of Naples in 1309, which covered much of southern Italy and some of southern France. Robert had a child by a previous marriage, but Sancia and Robert had no children. Sancia's brother, Philip, who had recently joined a strict branch of the Franciscans, the Fraticelli, came to live at court and gathered a group of strictly observant brothers around him. Sancia also had a group of Poor Clare nuns living at court with her.

The marriage initially was not smooth or happy. Robert was pre-occupied with military adventures and had a reputation for unfaith-fulness, while Sancia focused on the spiritual life. By 1316 Sancia wrote to the Pope requesting a divorce, but this was denied her. However, by the 1320s Robert too was focusing more on the life of the spirit, taking part in theological debates and even preaching. He shared Sancia's support of the Franciscan family in their kingdom and more widely, although their support of the Fraticelli, who saw themselves as the only legitimate followers of Francis, caused some problems in the wider church.

When Robert died in 1343, Sancia became regent of the kingdom for her step-granddaughter Joanna, daughter of Robert's son by his first marriage. The Council ruling alongside her was ineffective, however, and within the year the Pope imposed direct rule, and Sancia was at last free to become a Poor Clare nun in Naples, where she died 18 months later, aged about 60. While her life on the surface had not been difficult, she had struggled with a problem many face – how to combine a deep spiritual life with the duties of family and, in a sense, a working life. Darleen Pryds concludes:

> She did as many laywomen learn to do even today; she accommodated the particular life she found herself in to fit her innermost call and adapted her innermost call to fit within the royal life she was born into. In short, she crafted a life that she could claim was authentically her own.[94]

Alongside Sancia at the court of Naples was another woman who shaped her initial life of privilege into one of prayer, asceticism and charity through embracing the Franciscan way. Her name was **Delphine**, and she is remembered along with her husband, **Elzear**. Both of noble families, they were married in 1300 but, according to tradition, remained celibate. Elzear served at court, while Delphine became lady-in-waiting to the queen. Under the influence of Franciscan friars, they joined the Third Order around 1316. When Elzear died in 1328, Delphine remained at court as a close confidant of Sancia. Eventually she returned to her native Provence, living as a penitent recluse until her death in 1358. Like Sancia, she and Elzear had made a conscious decision to shape their life of privilege by different values.

Our next simple follower came from a very different background. **Didacus of Alcala** was born in 1400 to a poor family in the Andalusian region of Spain. After some time as a wandering hermit, he joined the friars as a lay brother and worked with his hands to help support the community. He also had a ministry of preaching. After some time he was sent to the Canary Islands, which had been part of Spain for only 40 years and were still mission territory. Initially he was porter of the friary, but in 1445 he was appointed as guardian, an unusual post for a lay brother.

In 1450 Didacus went to Rome to be present at the canonisation of Bernardine of Siena, whom we met in chapter 7. The arrival of many thousands of pilgrims led to an epidemic in the city, and he spent three months caring for the sick and praying for them. Many were cured through his prayer and his devoted care. From Rome he returned to Spain and spent the last years of his life in Alcala, living a life of solitude and contemplation, until his death in 1463. Following a number of miracles of healing attributed to his intercession, he was canonised in 1588, the first lay brother to be so honoured.

One of the miracles was the healing of Don Carlos, son of Philip II of Spain. Don Carlos led a rather riotous life, and after one night out he fell down the stairs and landed on his head. He was partially paralysed and became blind. He asked to pray to Didacus, and as a result the saint's body was brought to him. Don Carlos fell asleep with a hand on the friar's chest, and when he woke he told of a dream in which Didacus had assured him he would recover, and indeed he did. His grateful father commissioned a skilled mechanic to build a clockwork model of Didacus praying, which can still be seen in the Smithsonian Institution – a somewhat unusual tribute![95] This dramatic end to Didacus' story should not veil the simple life of a friar who went where he was asked to go, did whatever work he was given, whether humble or apparently important, and fulfilled the vocation he had believed in since he was a child.

Didacus followed one path for his entire life; **Sebastian de Aparicio**, on the other hand, changed tack, and he is perhaps an example of it never being too late to embrace a new way of life. Like Didacus, Sebastian was born into a poor Spanish family, in 1502, and worked as a migrant agricultural labourer before travelling to Mexico, then known as New Spain, in the hope of a better life. He arrived in 1533, worked as a rancher and then saw an opportunity as new towns were being built, and he became a road builder to connect them. He became very wealthy as a result of this clever move but continued to live simply, and after a time he returned to ranching, becoming known for his commitment to prayer and to charitable outreach.

In 1574 his second wife died, and at the age of 72 he asked to become a friar; he was accepted and spent most of the rest of his life as one of the friars who went out seeking alms for a large friary in Puebla, the town in which he had initially settled 40 years earlier. This job would have taken him out of the friary and given him many opportunities for ministry, and undoubtedly his varied life would have given him a wisdom which endeared him to those he met. He died aged 98 in 1600, having enjoyed good health until almost the end.

Seeking alms was also the ministry entrusted to **Felix of Cantalice**, born to a poor Italian family in 1515. He worked as a shepherd and then as a ploughman, until an accident in which he was trampled by a team of oxen caused him to think differently about his life. In 1543 he became a lay Franciscan friar. Five years later he was sent to Rome, and for the next 40 years he went out each day to beg for food and other alms to support the brothers. He was allowed to share what he gathered with the poor people of the streets, and this barefoot figure, often singing improvised songs, became much loved. He told stories to the children, who called him Brother Deo Gratias because he would always say 'Thanks be to God' when he was given alms.

His simplicity was also seen in his directness. He advised the preachers of his order to 'preach in order to convert people, not to make a name for yourselves'.[96] And when one of the brothers was elected pope, as Sixtus V, Felix advised him, 'When you become Pope, be Pope for the glory of God and the good of the church. Otherwise, it would be better for you to remain a simple friar.'[97] Philip Neri, founder of the Oratorians, a community for priests, often came to ask his advice, and they became close friends. Felix died in 1587 and was canonised in 1712. Almost three centuries after his death, his example inspired one of the largest congregations of Franciscan sisters, the Felician sisters, founded in Poland in the 1850s.

Benedict the Black had an even more unpromising start in life than Felix and Didacus. His parents were African slaves near Palermo, Sicily, though because of their good service to their master, Benedict himself was declared free at birth. But poverty prevented him from going to school, and he never learned to read or write. He became a shepherd and devoted himself to prayer, but even in this humble life the colour of his skin made him subject to bullying and insults. When he was 21, a nobleman saw how he remained patient in the face of this discrimination and invited Benedict to join him in forming a group of lay Franciscan hermits. Benedict first served as the cook, but eventually became the leader of the group.

After almost 20 years of this life, a papal edict ordered such groups of hermits to join an official religious order, so Benedict joined the friars in Palermo, where he once again became the cook. He accepted this return to humble service, but his dedication to the Rule and his spiritual gifts led to him being made novice master and then guardian, despite his illiteracy. After his terms in these jobs came to an end, he happily returned to his work as a cook. In Palermo, he had a reputation for wise spiritual guidance and for gifts of healing. He died there in 1589.

Another Italian-born friar from a humble background is **Humilis of Bisignano**. Born in 1582 in Calabria and baptised Luca Antonio, he worked as a farm labourer before joining the friars aged 27 as a lay brother. He was given the name Humilis (humble) because of how he related humbly to others in his daily work of caring for the friary and seeking alms. The deep prayer life that he had developed as a child continued to intensify, and he was blessed with many spiritual gifts, including the ability to read hearts and to prophesy. Perhaps the most striking was that of theological knowledge. Although he was illiterate and uneducated, he responded with great accuracy to questions on the scriptures and theology. This caused suspicion, and the church authorities investigated and interrogated him. But his wisdom surprised them all, and they were convinced that his knowledge came from God.

When Humilis lived for some time in Rome, he was the confidant and advisor of two popes, and the minister general took him as a companion when he visited the friars of Calabria and Sicily. He died in 1637 and was canonised in 2002. Pope John Paul II said of him:

> Humilis of Bisignano, invited by Christ to leave all and to risk all for the Kingdom of God, felt the fascination of the Gospel of the beatitudes and accepted to put himself at the service of the plan of God for him.[98]

It was this simple, and this demanding.

In the 19th century, a Bavarian brother, **Conrad of Parzham**, had a similar attitude. Born in 1818, he worked on the family farm until he was 31, when his father died (his mother had already died when he was 14) and he joined the Franciscans. He spent over 40 years as porter of his friary, which cared for the national Bavarian shrine of Mary. It was a busy life, but in the midst of all his duties, welcoming pilgrims and ministering to the people of the town, especially the poor, he devoted himself to prayer. He had a special love of silence; whenever he had spare time during the day he retreated to a nook near the door from which he could see the Blessed Sacrament in the church, and he would cut short his hours of sleep to continue to pray. He wrote in a letter:

> It is such a beautiful experience to converse with the good Lord. If we are truly recollected, nothing can stand in our way, even in the midst of the work our vocation requires of us. We will come to love silence, because whoever talks much will never arrive at a truly interior life.[99]

Our final follower certainly had serious work to attend to. **Pope John XXIII** may seem an unlikely person to include in this chapter. Elected pope in 1958, he is best known for summoning the Second Vatican Council, which opened in 1962 and was a landmark gathering in the life of the Catholic church, encouraging a return to the sources of faith at the same time as an openness to the modern world, to other churches and to other faiths. He was also a Franciscan.

Born as Angelo Guiseppe Roncalli to a poor Italian farming family in Baccanello, he said later that he had always been a Franciscan. When his family opened their window in the morning, the church that they saw was the Franciscan one, just down the street, and he became a member of the Third Order as a teenager. Throughout a long and eminent career in the church he always loved to return to Baccanello, and when he visited another friary after becoming pope he said, 'At one time I thought of following the humble friars of Baccanello, but then a stronger wind blew me on another road.'[100] At a papal audience with a group of friars, he told them, 'I wanted to put the friars minor last on my audience list to be able to enjoy their presence a bit longer.'[101]

Although the wind of God blew him to another road, his short time as pope encompassed many Franciscan themes, and his calling of the Second Vatican Council could certainly be seen as his response to the call of Christ to Francis, 'Go, rebuild my house!' Although Pope John XXIII died in 1963 and his successor continued the work of the council, this humbly Franciscan pope set its tone of engagement with God's world and of commitment to peace and justice. Perhaps God knew what he was doing in calling the young Angelo Guiseppe to follow a different road.

For reflection

- How do you wrestle with tensions between family ties and calling? Are there examples in this chapter (and others) to help as models?

- Is it ever too late to change your way of life? Do we expect and enable older people to do so?

- Are you, or might you be, willing to start again in a new life, even if it meant giving up much of the security or status which you have gained? Is there something you would love to do, if you had the courage? Take this into prayer and see what emerges.

- Go back to the questions at the end of chapter 1. What have you learnt from the followers of Christ in the ways of Francis and Clare whom you've met in this book? Spend some time in prayer asking God to show you 'what is yours to do'.

NOTES

1 Regis J. Armstrong, J.A. Wayne Hellman and William J. Short (eds), *Francis of Assisi: Early documents, Vol. 2: The Founder* (New City Press, 2000), p. 386.

2 Susan R. Pitchford, *The Sacred Gaze: Contemplation and the healing of the self* (Liturgical Press, 2014), p. 133.

3 Regis J. Armstrong, J.A. Wayne Hellman and William J. Short (eds), *Francis of Assisi: Early documents, Vol. 1: The Saint* (New City Press, 1999), p. 97.

4 Armstrong, Hellman and Short, *Francis of Assisi, Vol. 2*, p. 209.

5 Armstrong, Hellman and Short, *Francis of Assisi, Vol. 1*, p. 107.

6 Armstrong, Hellman and Short, *Francis of Assisi, Vol. 1*, p. 107. The quotation is from the Rule.

7 Barrie Williams, *The Franciscan Revival in the Anglican Communion* (DLT, 1982), p. 53.

8 Austin, Nicholas Alan and Tristam SSF (eds), *A Sense of the Divine: A Franciscan reader for the Christian year* (Canterbury Press, 2001), p. 320 (hereafter *SoD*).

9 *SoD*, p. 319.

10 Petà Dunstan, 'Whatever happened to Brother Giles?', *franciscan*, 29:1, January 2017, p. 16.

11 Williams, *The Franciscan Revival in the Anglican Communion*, p. 108.

12 Williams, *The Franciscan Revival in the Anglican Communion*, p. 122.

13 Williams, *The Franciscan Revival in the Anglican Communion*, p. 120.

14 Petà Dunstan, *This Poor Sort: A history of the European province of the Society of St Francis* (DLT, 1997), p. 97.

15 Ilia Delio, *A Franciscan View of Creation: Learning to live in a sacramental world* (The Franciscan Institute, 2003), p. 22.

16 Delio, *A Franciscan View of Creation*, p. 27.

17 Ilia Delio, 'The renaissance of Franciscan theology: retrieving the tradition of the good', in *Spirit and Life: A journal of contemporary Franciscanism*, vol. 8: Franciscan Studies: the difference women are making (Franciscan Institute Publications, 1999), p. 21.

18 **web.archive.org/web/20130126151732/http://home.infionline.net/~ddisse/pirckhei.html**

19 See note 18.

20   Thomas Merton, *The Seven Storey Mountain: An autobiography of faith* (Harcourt, 1948).

21   Ilia Delio, *The Humility of God: A Franciscan perspective* (St Anthony Messenger Press, 2005), p. 2.

22   Richard Rohr OFM, '75 years of life', 20 March 2018, **cac.org/75-years-of-life-2018-03-20**.

23   Dana Greene, 'Seize the Franciscan moment, Rohr advises', *National Catholic Reporter*, 23 July 2014, **ncronline.org/books/2017/08/seize-franciscan-moment-rohr-advises**.

24   Delio, 'The renaissance of Franciscan theology', p. 32.

25   Margaret Carney, 'Franciscan women and the theological enterprise', in Kenan B. Osborne (ed.), *The History of Franciscan Theology* (Franciscan Institute, 1994), p. 335.

26   Angela of Foligno, *Memorial*, quoted in William J. Short, *Poverty and Joy: The Franciscan tradition* (DLT, 1999), p. 106.

27   *SoD*, p. 94.

28   Short, *Poverty and Joy*, p. 49.

29   Short, *Poverty and Joy*, p. 49.

30   *SoD*, p. 305.

31   Short, *Poverty and Joy*, p. 49.

32   Regis J. Armstrong, J.A. Wayne Hellman and William J. Short (eds), *Francis of Assisi: Early documents, Vol. 3: The Prophet* (New City Press, 2001), p. 873.

33   *SoD*, p. 391.

34   David Bryant, 'Screaming tongues and silent aching', *Church Times*, 13 May 2016, **churchtimes.co.uk/articles/2016/13-may/faith/faith-features/screaming-tongues-and-silent-aching**.

35   Short, *Poverty and Joy*, p. 110.

36   Short, *Poverty and Joy*, p. 110.

37   Mauro Jöhri, 'The 350th anniversary of the birth of Saint Veronica Giuliani', *Curia Generalis Fratrum Minorum Capuccinorum*, circular letter no. 9, 2011, **web.archive.org/web/20120803111744/http://www.db.ofmcap.org:80/ofmcap/allegati/2316/circolare09_en.pdf**, p. 3.

38   Frère Marc, *J'ai dit oui au seigneur: La vie de Soeur Claire de l'Eucharistie* ['I said yes to the Lord: The life of Sister Claire of the Eucharist'] (Editions du Lion de Juda, 1986), p. 37 (my translation).

39   Marc, *J'ai dit oui au seigneur*, p. 46.

40   Marc, *J'ai dit oui au seigneur*, p. 61.

41   Marc, *J'ai dit oui au seigneur*, p. 105.

42   Marc, *J'ai dit oui au seigneur*, p. 124.
43   Marc, *J'ai dit oui au seigneur*, p. 124.
44   Marc, *J'ai dit oui au seigneur*, pp. 136–7.
45   Gwenfryd Mary CSF, 'RIP – Gabriel CSF', **franciscans.org.uk/ franciscan/obituary-notices/rip-gabriel-csf**.
46   Arthur Howells, *A Franciscan Way of Life: Brother Ramon's quest for holiness* (BRF, 2018), p. 11.
47   Ieuan Lloyd, 'RIP – Ramon SSF', **franciscans.org.uk/franciscan/ obituary-notices/rip-ramon-ssf**.
48   Darleen Pryds, *Women of the Streets: Early Franciscan women and their mendicant vocation* (Franciscan Institute, 2016), p. 47.
49   *SoD*, p. 382.
50   Christopher de Hamel, *Meetings with Remarkable Manuscripts* (Penguin, 2018), pp. 394–96.
51   Franciscan Intellectual Tradition, Facebook post, 5 July 2016, **facebook.com/franciscantradition/posts/603355239819749**.
52   Solange de Santis, 'Lambeth bishops attend closing Eucharist; martyred Melanesian brothers honored in Canterbury Cathedral', 3 August 2008, **archive.episcopalchurch.org/79901_99702_ENG_ HTM.htm**.
53   Querciolo Mazzonis, 'A female idea of religious perfection: Angela Merici and the Company of St Ursula (1535–40)', *Renaissance Studies*, 18:3 (2004), p. 403.
54   Samuel SSF, 'RIP – Colin Wilfred SSF', 4 September 2012, **franciscans. org.uk/franciscan/obituary-notices/rip-colin-wilfred-ssf**.
55   **johnbradburne.com**
56   **franciscansinternational.org/home**
57   Order of Friars Minor, 'Message of the minister general for the Week of Prayer for Christian Unity 2017', 27 December 2016, **ofm.org/ blog/message-of-the-minister-general-for-the-week-of-prayer-for- christian-unity-2017**.
58   **en.wikipedia.org/wiki/Religion_in_Japan**
59   **fmm-mysg.org/7-martyrs.html**
60   **en.wikipedia.org/wiki/Maria_Restituta_Kafka**
61   'World celebrates as two martyred friars beatified', *The St Anthony Companion*, March 2016, **newsletter.companionsofstanthony.org/ newsletters/2016-march/world-celebrates-as-two-martyred-friars- beatified**.
62   'World celebrates as two martyred friars beatified'.
63   **en.wikipedia.org/wiki/Mychal_Judge**

64   Jack Wintz OFM, 'Father Mychal Judge: Franciscan hero on 9/11',
      11 September 2017, **blog.franciscanmedia.org/franciscan-spirit/
      father-mychal-judge-franciscan-hero-on-9-11**.
65   See **i.ytimg.com/vi/ht3fGcso5JQ/maxresdefault.jpg**.
66   Wintz, 'Father Mychal Judge'.
67   **franciscantradition.org/blog/21-rose-of-viterbo**
68   L. Bressan, 'Odoric of Pordenone (1265–1331): his vision of China and
      South-East Asia and his contribution to relations between Asia and
      Europe', *Journal of the Malaysian Branch of the Royal Asiatic Society*,
      70:2 (1997), p. 4, **jstor.org/stable/41493334**.
69   Bressan, 'Odoric of Pordenone (1265–1331)', p. 10.
70   **quisestlullus.narpan.net/eng/1_intro_eng.html**
71   Franciscan Intellectual Tradition, Facebook post, 30 June 2018,
      facebook.com/franciscantradition/posts/978850462270223.
72   *SoD*, p. 337.
73   **vatican.va/spirit/documents/spirit_20010518_bernardino_
      en.html**, italics in original.
74   *SoD*, pp. 386–87.
75   A video of the statue is available at **youtube.com/
      watch?v=TJfyGArUr20**.
76   Thomas Reese, 'Junipero Serra: saint or not?', *National Catholic
      Reporter*, 15 May 2015, **ncronline.org/blogs/faith-and-justice/
      junipero-serra-saint-or-not**.
77   Reese, 'Junipero Serra'.
78   **fmmii.org/blessed-maria-assunta.html**
79   Armstrong, Hellman and Short, *Francis of Assisi, Vol. 1*, p. 74.
80   Franciscan Intellectual Tradition, Facebook post, 23 April 2018,
      facebook.com/franciscantradition/posts/934842246671045.
81   Andre Cirino OFM and Josef Raischl (eds), *Franciscan Solitude* (The
      Franciscan Institute, 1995), p. 253.
82   John Paul II, 'Canonization of 4 Blesseds', homily, 25 November 2001,
      **w2.vatican.va/content/john-paul-ii/en/homilies/2001/documents/
      hf_jp-ii_hom_20011125_canonization.html**.
83   *SoD*, p. 345.
84   *SoD*, p. 348.
85   *SoD*, p. 329.
86   *SoD*, p. 329.
87   *SoD*, p. 329.
88   Tim Wilson, 'Padre Pio introduced a doubt in my disbelief',
      23 February 2017, **animate-tim.com/2017/02/23/padre-pio-
      introduced-a-doubt-in-my-disbelief**.

89   en.wikipedia.org/wiki/Padre_Pio

90   solanuscasey.org/who-is-father-solanus/spirituality

91   solanuscasey.org/who-is-father-solanus/the-message

92   Howells, *A Franciscan Way of Life*, p. 11.

93   Frances Young, *God's Presence: A contemporary recapitulation of early Christianity* (Cambridge University Press, 2013), p. 337.

94   Pryds, *Women of the Streets*, p. 65.

95   Elizabeth King, 'Clockwork prayer: a sixteenth-century mechanical monk', *Blackbird: an online journal of literature and the arts* 1:1 (2002), blackbird.vcu.edu/v1n1/nonfiction/king_e/prayer_introduction.htm.

96   *SoD*, p. 333.

97   *SoD*, p. 333.

98   vatican.va/news_services/liturgy/2002/documents/ns_lit_doc_20020519_umile_en.html

99   *SoD*, p. 325.

100 André Cirino OFM, 'Saint John XXIII, secular Franciscan', *TAU-USA* 79 (Spring 2014), pp. 20–21, nafra-sfo.org/tau-usa/articles/spring14/feature1_spring14.pdf.

101 Cirino, 'Saint John XXIII, secular Franciscan'.

BIBLIOGRAPHY AND FURTHER READING

Regis J. Armstrong OFM Cap (ed. and trans.), *Clare of Assisi: Early documents* (Paulist Press, 1988).

Regis J. Armstrong, *St Francis of Assisi: Writings for a gospel life* (St Paul's, 1994) – uses Francis' writings to reflect on gospel living.

Regis J. Armstrong OFM Cap, J. A. Wayne Hellman OFM Conv and William J. Short OFM (eds), *Francis of Assisi: Early documents. Vol. I: The Saint. Vol. II: The Founder. Vol. III: The Prophet* (New City Press, 1999–2001).

Regis Armstrong OFM Cap and Ignatius Brady OFM, *Francis and Clare: The complete works* (Paulist Press, 1982).

Austin, Nicholas Alan and Tristam SSF (eds), *A Sense of the Divine: A Franciscan reader for the Christian year* (Canterbury Press, 2001).

Andre Cirino OFM and Josef Raischl (eds), *Franciscan Solitude* (The Franciscan Institute, 1995).

Mark Davis and Francis Cotter OFM, *Glimpses of the Franciscan Way* (Rockpool Publishing, 2012) – a very attractive pictorial presentation of the Franciscan way, with real wisdom in its short text.

Ilia Delio OSF et al. *Care for Creation: A Franciscan spirituality of the earth* (Franciscan Media, 2009) – environmental science, Franciscan spirituality and reflective action.

Ilia Delio OSF, *Clare of Assisi: A heart full of love* (St Anthony Messenger Press, 2007).

Ilia Delio OSF, *Franciscan Prayer* (St Anthony Messenger Press, 2004).

Ilia Delio OSF, *A Franciscan View of Creation: Learning to live in a sacramental world* (The Franciscan Institute, 2003).

Ilia Delio OSF, *The Humility of God: A Franciscan perspective* (St Anthony Messenger Press, 2005).

Ilia Delio OSF, 'The renaissance of Franciscan theology: retrieving the tradition of the good', in *Spirit and Life: A journal of contemporary*

Franciscanism, Vol. 8 – Franciscan Studies: The difference women are making (Franciscan Institute Publications, 1999), pp. 21–41.

Ilia Delio OSF, *Simply Bonaventure: An introduction to his life, thought and writing* (second edition, New City Press, 2013).

Peta Dunstan, *This Poor Sort: A history of the European province of the Society of St Francis* (DLT, 1997).

Elizabeth CSF, *Corn of Wheat: The life and history of the Community of St Francis* (Becket Publications, 1981).

Helen Julian CSF, *Living the Gospel: The spirituality of St Francis and St Clare* (BRF, 2001).

Arthur Howells, *A Franciscan Way of Life: Brother Ramon's quest for holiness* (BRF, 2018).

William R Hugo OFM Cap, *Studying the Life of Saint Francis of Assisi: A beginner's workbook* (second edition, New City Press, 2011) – provides tools for the reader to engage with the documents on Francis, looking at the sources through the lens of history.

Mary Beth Ingham CSJ, *Scotus for Dunces: An introduction to the Subtle Doctor* (Franciscan Institute Publications, 2003).

Damian Kirkpatrick SSF, Philip Doherty OFM Conv and Shelagh O'Flynn FMDM (eds), *Joy in All Things: A Franciscan companion* (Canterbury Press, 2002).

Frère Marc, *J'ai dit oui au seigneur: la vie de Soeur Claire de l'Eucharistie* (Editions du Lion de Juda, 1986).

Dawn M Northwehr OSF, *The Franciscan View of the Human Person: Some central elements* (The Franciscan Institute, 2005).

Kenan B Osborne OFM, *The Franciscan Intellectual Tradition: Tracings its origins and identifying its central components* (The Franciscan Institute, 2003).

Kenan B Osborne OFM (ed.), *The History of Franciscan Theology* (Franciscan Institute, 1994).

Susan Pitchford, *Following Francis: The Franciscan way for everyone* (Morehouse Publishing, 2006) – an American Third Order member writes about her journey of exploration into the Franciscan way.

Darleen Pryds, *Women of the Streets: Early Franciscan women and their mendicant vocation*, 'Franciscan Heritage Series' vol. 7 (Franciscan Institute, 2016).

Br Ramon SSF, *Franciscan Spirituality: Following St Francis today*, (second edition, SPCK, 2008).

Richard Rohr, *Eager to Love: The alternative way of Francis of Assisi* (Hodder and Stoughton, 2014).

Richard Rohr OFM with John Feister, *Hope against Darkness: The transforming vision of Saint Francis in an age of anxiety* (St Anthony Messenger Press, 2001).

William J. Short OFM, *Poverty and Joy: The Franciscan tradition* (DLT, 1999).

Helen Stanton, *For Peace and For Good: A history of the European province of the Community of St Francis* (Canterbury Press, 2017).

Barrie Williams, *The Franciscan Revival in the Anglican Communion* (DLT, 1982).

Rowan Clare Williams, *A Condition of Complete Simplicity: Franciscan wisdom for today's world* (Canterbury Press, 2003).

Websites

catholicapologetics.info/library/onlinelibrary/Opus.pdf – a PDF of the Writings of St Francis translated from the 1976 Critical Latin Edition of Fr Katejan Esser, OFM, with introduction and notes.

franciscans.org.uk – the Anglican Franciscans in the UK has more on Francis, Clare and Franciscan life, as well as a useful collection of links.

www.franciscanpublications.com – Franciscan Institute Publications publishes a wide range of books on Franciscan topics, in various series. The 'Franciscan Heritage' series provides especially useful brief introductions to various subjects, such as creation, the Trinity and beauty.

franciscantradition.org – the Franciscan Intellectual Tradition; a very useful resource for anyone interested in bringing the spiritual heritage of Francis and Clare to people today. The resources include the writings of Francis and Clare.

slr-ofs.org/st-clares-letters-to-st-agnes-of-prague.html – the letters of St Clare to St Agnes, with introduction.

frere-rufin.com/pages/en/claire/ecrits-sainte-claire – the writings of St Clare, without commentary or notes.